AF413648

Testimonials

"Few entrepreneurs have built empires with as much heart and success as John Paul DeJoria. From twice experiencing homelessness to scaling billion-dollar businesses, John Paul never forgot the importance of generosity and sharing his success with others. *Success Unshared is Failure* is a captivating telling of his own story, in his own words—and a perfect read for anyone looking for inspiration."

— **Tony Robbins**, America's #1 Life and Business Strategist, *New York Times* Best-Selling author

———— ❋ ————

"This is storytelling at its finest...raw, real, and relentlessly hopeful. John Paul invites you into the moments that shaped him, showing that the road to lasting success is paved with compassion, grit, and a belief that we rise highest when we lift others."

— **Jeff Bloomfield**, Award-Winning Author & World-Renowned Leadership and Communication Speaker

———— ❋ ————

"John Paul DeJoria is a man whose life has been shaped by his generous heart and soul, hard work, and mighty dreaming as well as a passion for doing good things—for our earth, the animals, and humanity. This is a book that will inspire readers to live life to their fullest potential. A joy of a book to read and a joy of a friend to know."

—**Pierce Brosnan**, OBE Actor, Producer, Artist, Activist . . .

"John Paul DeJoria embodies the spirit of generosity, resilience, and purpose-driven leadership. His life story is a testament to the power of believing in yourself and lifting others as you rise. JP's philosophy, 'Success Unshared is Failure,' is not just a slogan— it's a way of life. He has made it his mission to share his success by mentoring young entrepreneurs, investing in people from all walks of life, and creating opportunities for those who might otherwise be overlooked. Through his philanthropic foundation and hands-on involvement, JP works tirelessly to build an inclusive world where everyone, regardless of background, has a chance to thrive. JP proves that true happiness and success come from helping others and making a positive impact wherever you go."

— **Meena Lakdawala-Flynn**
Partner, Goldman Sachs & Co.

"John Paul DeJoria has always demonstrated that true wealth and happiness is giving back, both to people and to our planet. His generous support for over 35 years has enabled us to launch and maintain three ships that have saved thousands of whales, dolphins, and seals. JP has been an incredible warrior for the protection of life in the Ocean."

— **Captain Paul Watson**
Founder, Paul Watson Foundation (2022)
Founder of Sea Shepherd (1977)

───────── ❊ ─────────

"JP's stories will inspire you to be more, do more and have more, and give more. He exemplifies what one person with desire, discipline, dedication, and determination can do to make great things happen, even when they seem impossible. Aristotle's 'Golden Mean Virtues' of courage, truthfulness, friendliness, liberty, generosity, and temperance are the way JP lives, moves, and expresses. If we're each coded with a destiny, JP has found the way to tap that code to flourish in his highest destiny. You won't be able to resist being deeply inspired by his journey. Simultaneously, making your life and destiny ever better, too."

— Mark Victor Hansen
59 times *New York Times*, best selling author

Success Unshared is Failure

JOHN PAUL DeJORIA

Success Unshared is Failure

A POST HILL PRESS BOOK,
PUBLISHED IN COOPERATION WITH MARK VICTOR HANSEN LIBRARY

ISBN: 979-8-89565-640-2
ISBN (eBook): 979-8-89565-641-9

Creative contribution by Veronica Deisler and Carol McManus
Cover design by JPMS Creative Marketing Team
Cover photo by Estelle Bohl
Interior layout by DBree

This is a work of nonfiction. All people, locations, events, and situations are portrayed to the best of the author's memory.

This book, as well as any other Post Hill Press publications, may be purchased in bulk quantities at a special discounted rate. Contact orders@posthillpress.com for more information.

Post Hill Press
New York • Nashville
posthillpress.com

Printed and bound in China
Published in the United States of America
1 2 3 4 5 6 7 8 9 10

This book is dedicated to my wonderful mother, Yvonne Madelo DeJoria, who had little but gave me and others so much.

Me and mom dancing; Ballroom dance was one of her passions!

Photo courtesy of author's personal collection

TABLE OF CONTENTS

Foreword
by Mark Victor Hansen

Like a caterpillar transforms into a chrysalis before becoming a butterfly, John Paul DeJoria has an uncanny ability to take life's tragedies and turn them into triumphs. He was homeless twice and overcame these and many more adversities transforming himself into a business maverick who became a multi-billionaire.

It has been my great pleasure to know "JP", as he is affectionately called, since we were introduced by a mutual friend in the mid-90s. The first time we met, we quickly realized we shared that same self-driven passion that comes from being a young man with immigrant parents who grew up never having quite enough. Coming from homes that provided only the basics, sometimes even less, imbued an early entrepreneurial spirit in each of us leading to what most would consider impossible success for men of such humble backgrounds.

My first meeting with JP was at his beautiful Malibu Beach home. Before that meeting I knew him only as the happy face seen on Paul Mitchell television commercials all over the world. John Paul was a global icon to women and stylists who wanted the highest quality products for their hair. He started John Paul Mitchell Systems with co-founder, Paul Mitchell, using their combined savings of only seven-hundred dollars together with infinite genius, and unstoppable work ethic.

Not only did JP own one of the top-selling hair care companies in the world, but he was also several years into his business venture with his enormously successful Patrón tequila.

Taking in the views of the beautiful Pacific Ocean, we shared a shot of tequila and got to know one another, swapping stories of each of us building ourselves and our giant business operations. We both started with virtually nothing except a deep desire to achieve far beyond the limits of our early years.

The similarities of our respective early lives were uncanny. JP and I both sold greeting cards at age nine to earn our own money. We each had responsibility for a newspaper, route selling and delivering daily news. We'd both done door-to-door sales—he peddled encyclopedias, I cable services.

As we created giant enterprises out of our own ideas and tireless work, the results of those activities fueled another similar fire in each of us—the passion to give back and make the world a better place.

JP and I have been friends and colleagues now for over three decades. When running a hundred-million-dollar seminar company, "The Enlightened Millionaire Institute," I frequently asked JP to come and speak. He never failed to enthrall the attendees, sharing his journey of success that epitomizes the American dream of creating something really special from nothing, then using those resources to make positive impact for the good of all. People attending those events would wait long periods of time to meet him and get a photo with the man they saw as a true legend.

JP dazzles audiences around the world with tales of his extraordinary life through speaking engagements and television interviews. He is always humble, insisting that his success is not because he is exceptional, but rather an example to inspire others. He believes that with white-hot desire anyone can achieve their dreams if they dedicate themselves to their pursuits.

I've watched JP through the years as he achieved one giant success after another, then parlayed them into more giving projects. I came to believe he has such an enormous spirit, that the universe responds equally, and in kind, to the largess of the goodness he embodies.

I watched him take Barbuda, a hurricane-ravaged island in the Caribbean, and bring it back to life by restoring the coral reefs and creating new employment for those who were forced to evacuate. He demonstrated what one on-purpose human being can accomplish.

Yeah Samake, one of the visionary leaders from Mali, West Africa, raved to me about John Paul's assistance in helping his starving people. By providing the resources to access enough water JP is feeding the populations in those villages and giving them the means to help themselves.

In Austin, Texas he partnered with a woman helping the homeless by providing resources to not only feed the hungry, but to help them find the path back to viable employment. The program is so successful that it has become a model for other cities to follow.

Within these pages, you'll read countless dramatic stories of JP overcoming adversity yet repeatedly coming out on top. With his triumphs, he realized that *Success Unshared is Failure*—his personal mantra naturally became the title of this book.

JP's philanthropic heart and deeds were recognized by one of the most prestigious awards given to philanthropists—

The Horatio Alger Award for Distinguished Americans. It was awarded to JP at the United States Supreme Court by Justice Clarence Thomas. The award recognizes exceptional people who came from rags to riches and have been excessively philanthropic. Horatio Alger has granted over thirty-seven thousand scholarships to at-risk students, valued at over two-hundred-sixty-five-million dollars for college, university, or technical school tuition.

JP and I have each received this rare and highly coveted award becoming Horatio Alger Association members. Yet, another uncanny parallel where the journeys of our lives have intertwined.

In life, there are givers and takers. John Paul DeJoria is a master giver, whom my wife Crystal and I love, respect, and admire. He truly epitomizes the title of this book and personifies what the master Jesus said, "It is more blessed to give, than receive." He has the heart, mind, and soul of a giver—one that has been magnificently blessed. JP has decided to keep on giving until the giver of all takes him lovingly home to heaven.

It has been my great honor to publish this book about one of the more extraordinary men of our time. I predict it will become a favorite in your library—a treasure that provides a template for living life to your fullest expression of joy and success.

— Mark Victor Hansen
59 times #1 NYT's bestselling author
Chicken Soup for the Soul®

Eloise, me, Robert Kennedy Jr., Crystal and Mark Victor Hansen
Photo courtesy of Mark Victor Hansen

Introduction

The title of this book means a lot to me. It's a philosophy my mother taught me when I was a boy, and my business partner and I practiced it as we built John Paul Mitchell Systems. It's also an idea I've come to believe in even more deeply today. When I say *"success unshared is failure"* I mean this: when you do better at something than you were doing before, helping other people should be part of what you do now. When you get rewarded for your efforts—and that doesn't always mean money—I feel you need to share your good luck. Sharing expands your reach. It expands your frequency. If you're fortunate enough to succeed in anything and just keep it to yourself, that's failure. You probably won't be as happy a person if you don't see the benefit in bringing others up along with you.

For us, that meant designing a company that supported the needs of hairdressers. With their help, we created our company to include hairdressers in our activities and decisions from day one. Our products are designed with hairdressers in mind. We include them in our marketing and charitable activities. And we take care of our hairdressers when times are tough. As the Paul Mitchell Schools got going, we included our students, too.

The company we started, with just seven hundred dollars, became the largest independently-owned professional hair care company, and we're in over one hundred countries worldwide. This turned out to be my first billion-dollar company opportunity.

My success with John Paul Mitchell Systems has also given me the financial means to spread my philosophy throughout the world. You'll read in this book how I've invested in companies that span from providing food and water to people who need it most, to partnerships that will help to save the future of our beautiful earth. I've gotten involved with many projects simply because they touch my heart and make me want to help others live better lives.

My philosophy, *"success unshared is failure,"* has brought me great happiness. I hope it will inspire you to take it as your own. You don't have to be wealthy to make it work for you. There are more ways than one to be successful. My mother taught me that no matter how badly off you think you are, someone else is facing even greater challenges, and you won't be really happy unless you find a way to help them. That's the message I want to pass on.

When I look back at what led up to my starting the company with my brilliant hairstylist partner, Cyril Thomson Mitchell (Paul Mitchell), it's hard to believe my prior beauty industry experience included getting fired three times. Of course, without that happening, John Paul Mitchell Systems wouldn't be what it is today. Neither would I. And neither would the people I've helped. Faith is real.

— John Paul DeJoria

Chapter 1

Believe in Yourself and
You *Will* Succeed

L et's start at the beginning. It's important to start there, because most everything I am and all I believe came from the woman who raised me, Yvonne Madelo DeJoria.

Me, Mom, and my older brother Robert in front of our Echo Park home
Photo courtesy of author's personal collection

My mother immigrated from Greece and eventually married my father who was of European descent. I was born in 1944, less than two years after my older brother, Robert Anthony DeJoria. My parents separated before I was two and I never got to know my father. It wasn't easy for my mom to raise two boys on her own, but she managed. I learned a lot from my mom. She taught us that happiness is what makes you wealthy.

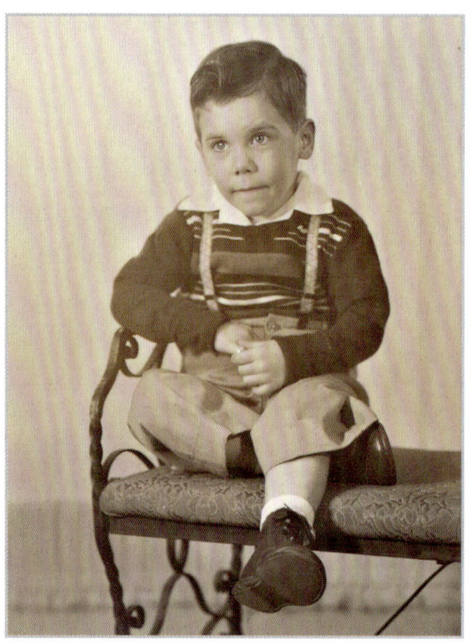

Me, about 3 years old
Photo courtesy of author's personal collection

We didn't have a lot, but we didn't know it. We had a couple of changes of clothes. We'd wear shoes until the soles got holes in them, then we'd patch the holes with cardboard, and cover it with black shoe polish so the other kids wouldn't make fun of us as we walked up the stairs at school.

At one time, our family fortune consisted of twenty-seven cents. I remember that day so clearly; it was a Friday. Even with twenty-seven cents to her name, Mom said we were rich because the bills were paid, we had each other, and we had food in the icebox. (Yes, we had one of those in the early days, before we bought a refrigerator. The iceman would come along and put a big block of ice in there.) We were happy, so we were rich.

Mom inspired us to want to help others. When we were little, we lived in a small one-bedroom house in Echo Park, near Los Angeles. It wasn't a wealthy neighborhood, but a nice place to live. Most of our neighbors were European immigrants. We didn't have a lot of money, so it was a big deal at Christmas time when our mom took us downtown to see the decorations at the big department stores. They had puppets that moved, trains running around their tracks, and all kinds of fun toys. Each year, we looked forward to spending an entire evening in front of the glass windows of Bullocks, Broadway, and May Company, *oohing* and *aahing* over the scenes. We'd get on the electric trolley car for a nickel apiece, and off we'd go.

One Christmas, when I was about six years old, Mom gave my brother and me a single dime. She told us each to hold onto half of it, walk over to the person ringing the bell, and put that dime in the red bucket. We did it, of course, but not without asking why. After all, a dime was a lot of money in the early 1950s. It could buy two candy bars, two soft drinks—it could buy so many things!

"Don't we need that money?" we asked.

"Yes, we do," Mom said. "But I wanted you to know something about life. Always remember, boys, no matter what we have, and no matter where you go in life, there's always someone worse off than you and they need your help. That's the Salvation Army; they help people who don't have food or a place to live, and we're going to help them with our dime." These words have stayed with me all my life:

Success Unshared is Failure

That experience also showed that sharing is the only way to go. My mom also taught me this: If I have a cookie and cut it in half, I should give the bigger half to my friend and eat the smaller half. What's the end result? Not only are you sharing, but your friend knows that you really care about him and that you are kind. Even in (what some call) my bad-ass, biker-dude days during my twenties when we didn't have much money, I'd take my young son (he was two or three years old at the time) to help serve food at the Thanksgiving and Christmas feed-ins at Griffith Park in Los Angeles. We didn't have much to give, but that was our way of giving back.

Robert and Me in Crestline
Photo courtesy of author's personal collection

People can give back by taking the time to do something for somebody else. It can be as easy as mowing a lawn for an elderly neighbor who's low on money. It costs you nothing to do it. Every time you do something out of your own heart to help others, it expands your heart even bigger. When you give back, it makes you feel really good, especially if you give back without asking for anything in return. If you ask for something in return, you're not really giving—you're trading.

Be Careful What You Wish For

My mom, who had an accent, still connected with everybody extremely well. She was amazing. She took great care of me and my brother and taught us how to be better people. She had a little backyard vegetable garden where we'd grow our own string beans, carrots, celery, lettuce, beets, and whatever else we could. She was Greek so she brought that with her over the ocean from her homeland.

In the forties and fifties she worked for a company designing and making hats. From five-years-old until nine, because she had to work Monday through Friday to support us, we stayed in a foster home during the week with a family in East L.A. They weren't especially loving, but we'd go home for weekends and get plenty of love from our incredible mom.

Some of my favorite memories growing up were from when she'd make a big deal out of a special treat. Once a month she'd bring home a very small slice of filet mignon or something like it and she'd cut it into three pieces. Once we even had a little caviar. It was inexpensive back then. She'd give us treats like that and say, "Boys, here's how the wealthy people eat, and we eat the same way." She was such a great mom.

Mom riding my tricycle ... she loved to have fun!
Photo courtesy of author's personal collection

Even when times were tough, we thought our childhood was fine. We didn't know any better. At Christmas, we usually got two presents each. We didn't know that other kids got five or ten. One year, my mom asked, "What do you boys want?"

My brother said skates or something like that, but yours truly said, "A baby elephant."

"Well, how about skates?" Mom asked.

"Ma, I really want a baby elephant."

Sure enough, one of my two presents that year was a ceramic baby elephant planter. Be careful what you wish for—it might come true!

Variety Boys Club

Sometime around 1950, when my brother and I were about eight and six years old, we discovered the Variety Boys Club. It was on Cincinnati Street in East Los Angeles and was a place to keep kids like us off the streets. We didn't know we were underprivileged, but that's what they said the Variety Boys Club was for—so apparently, we were. Not that it mattered because we sure loved that club! It had many fun activities, but what we loved most was hanging out after school and on Saturdays, talking to our pals, and making projects in the wood shop.

One of my favorite memories from that time was learning how to make a flower planter box. It was probably two feet long and oval-shaped, with a flat bottom and curved sides made from wooden slats that we attached with nails. It had two hooks, so you could hang it up or set it on a windowsill.

My brother and I paid twenty-five cents—on credit—for the materials and spent a few days making the best planter box anyone could make. We varnished, sanded, and took our time to produce a top-quality product (by a little kid's standards, of course). Even at that age, we figured that if we took a little extra time to make it really nice, someone would want to buy it. When we were done, we made the rounds in the neighborhood, looking for a customer. We walked into a little restaurant on Wabash Avenue and asked the people seated at the counter, "Would you like to buy this?"

A lot of people said no, but the waitress said, "Oh, I can use that! Here, boys, here's fifty cents." After going back to the club and paying the quarter we owed for the kit, that left us twenty-five cents profit—a small fortune, when you stop to think that a soda pop cost five cents at that time. We took our twenty-five-cent profit, made another planter, sold it and made a total fifty-cent profit!

The Variety Boys Club also took us kids to the mountains. Every year for about three or four years, we'd spend a week or so at this wonderful camp in the Angeles National Forest. We stayed in wooden cabins and took nature walks. Once we even saw a rattlesnake that had just eaten a meal. We learned to make braids out of pine needles and made lanyards out of plastic—all the usual things kids do at camp. Going to that wonderful camp was so much fun. I learned a lot about nature too.

Many years later, I was honored to help renovate the sixty-five-year-old Variety Boys Club building. Imagine my surprise when the staff gave me the very same workbench my brother and I used to build our planter box. It even had the same vise attached.

Me and Robert in Arrowhead
Photo courtesy of author's personal collection

World's Greatest Mini Christmas Card Salesman

Another way I made money as a kid was the time I became the world's greatest Mini-Christmas Card salesman . . . for an eight-and-a-half-year-old boy, that is. There was an ad on the back of a comic book that said something like, "Send us your name and we'll send you a free sample kit." Inside the kit were five or six different Christmas cards to show customers the design options and how to personalize them with their names. The idea was to take their orders, collect half the money, and send it in to pay for their cards. When the company filled the orders, I'd deliver the cards, collect the other half they owed, and keep it for my work.

For an eight-and-a-half-year-old kid, my sales strategy wasn't half bad. I'd draw some little Christmas cards and hold up a sample card, saying, "You can have a homemade card like this or a real good one like this!" Of course, they didn't want mine. Then came the real sales pitch: "Okay, they're only ten cents each. Can you order twenty?" Selling those cards was such a fun thing to do. I'd hit up all the neighbors, sell five or ten cards, and make a little cash. The thrill of the sale was just as important to me as the money I made.

The Pink Rats

Around that time—this was still before I was ten—I was in a little kids' street gang in East L.A. We weren't like the gangs of today. We were just little kids who thought we were cool. We called ourselves the Pink Rats (my brother came up with that name) and we painted a little pink rat with snarling teeth on our leather jackets. We'd meet by a tree on Stone Street, and that tree was like our clubhouse. After school, we'd all hang out there for a while before going home.

All of us Pink Rats carried push-button knives like in Marlon Brando's movie *The Wild Ones.* We bought them at the local hardware store. They were maybe two inches long when they were closed. We loved pulling them out, and we'd get into occasional fistfights, but we never thought of stabbing anyone. Lots of other kids were using pocket knives to write on trees or carve their initials into things. We never did that, especially to our tree. There weren't a lot of good trees in our neighborhood. Even at that age, we knew enough to appreciate and enjoy ours.

Our big claim to fame was that we could outrun a kid we called "Big Gabriel." As the nickname implied, he was a big kid with a big temper to match. But if he got mad at something we said, we knew we could outrun him . . . and we did! It was a valuable lesson at that point in time. I found out it's not necessarily the biggest guy who wins, sometimes it's the fastest.

Do What You Love, Love What You Do

When my brother and I were about eleven and nine years old, Mom bought a little two-bedroom house in the Los Angeles neighborhood of Atwater Village. The house probably cost about a thousand to two thousand dollars, but it seemed like a mansion compared to the tiny house we'd rented until then. Mom had saved up for years until she had five hundred dollars or so for the down payment on a mortgage she could afford. We got our first black and white TV there when I was eleven.

The next year, my brother and I got a newspaper route. We'd get up at four-thirty in the morning, seven days a week. We even had to fold the *Los Angeles Examiner* before we delivered it. All the money we earned from that route went to our mom. We made about thirty dollars a month—each.

Things were different in those days. We were proud to have a job and know we were contributing to our family. It wasn't about making money to buy stuff for us. Even then, as kids, we wanted to work and do more to help our mom.

We made a deal with the local *Examiner* distributor, saying, "If we can go out and get new customers for you, can we have a dollar per customer, plus a paper route?" He said, "Sure you can!" So, we'd do our best to get new subscriptions. We'd hold the newspaper up and show people the various sections. We never knew if it was our brilliant sales pitch or the fact that we bored them for three or four minutes, but they'd often say, "Okay, we'll take it, we'll take it!" Who knows? Maybe we made a decent presentation.

Selling the *Examiner* was easy because we believed in our product. Like most young kids, I really loved the "funny papers," as we called the comics back then. The *Examiner's* funnies included Alley Oop, Beetle Bailey—all the coolest characters!—so half my presentation was, "We have the best funny papers in the world!"

There wasn't a doubt in my mind—that paper was the best. What a valuable lesson for a young boy to learn:

When you do what you love, it's easy to be excited about your work.

When you do what you love, your work becomes a part of you, and it doesn't feel like a job. Whenever you give a presentation about your product or service, you can honestly talk about how much you believe in your product, and your excitement shows. When a job becomes just a job, you get bored and that comes across too.

Least Likely to Succeed

A dear friend of mine in high school was a really cool girl named Michelle Gilliam. We were never boyfriend and girlfriend, but we used to hang out and we were good pals. Michelle sat behind me in Mr. Wachs' eleventh-grade business class. One day, I wrote a note, leaned back, and passed it to Michelle. It was a typical, dopey, teenage note, something like: "Ronnie and Darlene are going to Winchell's after school. Do you want to go down there too?" But Mr. Wachs intercepted the note and read it out loud to the whole class. He told everyone, "See these two? Don't hang out with them. They'll never make it in business. Look at them. They're supposed to be here to learn but they're passing this stupid note. Don't hang out with them. They're not going to succeed at all."

Years later, my wife Eloise threw me a surprise 50th birthday party at El Cholo. Michelle found Mr. Wachs and brought him to it. He didn't recall saying that, but Michelle and I remembered it clearly. We told him, "By the way, three years later, Michelle was one of the biggest pop music stars in the world." In case you didn't recognize her name, Michelle Gilliam became Michelle Phillips, the successful singer, songwriter, and actress who gained fame as a member of The Mamas and The Papas.

Lucky for us, we didn't pay any attention to Mr. Wachs' prediction. It had absolutely no effect on us, because *we believed in ourselves*. We just needed to figure out better ways to pass our notes!

Success Means Doing Your Best, Even When No One Is Watching

Confidence is certainly important, but here's another key ingredient in the formula for success. Many people define success as being wealthy, but my definition of success is *how well you do what you do.*

As a sixteen-year-old kid working at Stewart's Cleaners during my junior year in high school, my job included putting the drapes and pant sleeves on the hangers, brushing the blankets, sweeping the place, and cleaning up. Whatever Stewart wanted, I did. Stewart was so cheap, he squeaked. He would have paid fifty cents an hour if he thought he could get away with it, but he had to pay the minimum wage of one dollar and twenty-five cents an hour—and I was happy to get it.

When she was raising my brother and me, my mom always had us do chores and help around the house. One week, my brother would do the dishes and I'd sweep the floors. The next week, we'd swap. We didn't just go through the motions; Mom taught us how to *really* clean. That meant moving the trash can out of the way and cleaning under it, not just around it. Putting the chairs upside down on top of the table to sweep the floor underneath. We figured everyone grew up that way. So, working at Stewart's Cleaners, that's the way I cleaned, because that's the way it was supposed to be done.

Stewart had a mezzanine level with file cabinets and a little metal cot with a mattress on it, where he could rest if he was tired or working late at night. One day Stewart said, "Johnnie, come here, I want to talk to you." (Everyone called me Johnnie in high school.)

Uh-oh, what did I do? I thought. Sure hope I'm not gonna lose this job. My family could really use this buck and a quarter an hour.

"Last night, I worked late," Stewart said. "I lay down on the cot and put my watch on the table next to it. The watch fell off when I got up, so I looked for it under the bed. I noticed that it was clean under there. No dirt, no dust."

He continued, "I moved the cot and looked behind the cabinets, too. There was no dust there, either. My gosh, you moved everything when you cleaned. Who told you to do that?"

"Nobody. You hired me to clean, to be the janitor, and I'm going to be the best darned janitor in the world. I love my job, and I love what I do."

"I'm giving you a twenty-five-cent an hour raise," Stewart said. Suddenly, my pay was one-dollar and fifty cents an hour, making me one of the highest-paid kids at John Marshall High and the happiest kid in the world. Whether you're a janitor like I was or doing anything else, success means doing your best at the job you have, even when nobody's watching.

It Helps When Others Believe In You Too

Another good friend in high school was a guy named Lee Meyer. We'd been friends since junior high and we hung out together all the time. We lived in the same neighborhood until his family moved to the San Fernando Valley, to a town called Pacoima, not too far from Atwater Village.

Since we didn't have enough money to buy a decent car, my brother bought a fixer upper, and I rebuilt it—engine and all—during three semesters of auto shop. One night, my buddies got together, and we filled that beautiful '52 Ford with six people. Off we went, driving through the hills and looking for some hermit we'd heard about. Crazy kids! It started to rain a bit and, as we drove down a hill, we hit a dirt patch that was wet on the top and dry on the bottom, sending the car spinning out of control. There were two choices available: go over the cliff or spin the wheel back and hit the side of the hill. I opted for the hill. Luckily, no one was hurt, but the car was badly wrecked. So back to our school's auto shop we went.

While the car was being repaired, Lee loaned me an old car with a broken axle. What a good friend he was! We towed that car to auto shop, too, where I fixed the broken axle and had a car to drive.

One day, I drove over to auto shop and parked Lee's car on a hill, setting the brake and shifting the gear into first. Somehow, the brake released itself and the car popped out of gear, sending it hurtling down the hill and smashing the whole front end.

"Lee, I'll pound it out, but it won't be like new," I sadly had to tell my friend.

"Johnnie, don't worry about it. These things happen," Lee said. "Just do the best you can." Lee was one bad-ass dude but a great guy with a heart of gold. He helped me out more than once in my life and was a wonderful example of how to treat people well and be a good friend. I never forgot this, and later in life I finally had the chance to repay his kindness by buying him a new car. I was also able to offer him the job of his choice at John Paul Mitchell Systems (hereafter referred to as JPMS), and he proudly became our traffic manager.

When you have great role models, supportive friends and family, and people to teach you to always do your best, self-confidence comes easily. It's no wonder it made such a difference in my future.

Me and my super cool friend, Lee Meyer

Chapter 2

Life's Misfortunes Can Teach You a Lot

Have you ever asked yourself, Why was I dealt such a lousy hand? Why are these things happening to me?

I believe that life's hardships can turn out to be blessings because they teach us what we need to know to get to the next step. Sometimes we're dealt a good hand, sometimes not so good, and sometimes we run into trouble. Rather than calling them disasters, maybe we choose to call them "things that happened in the past that were kind of unfortunate but made us who we are today."

Do my past adversities haunt me? Absolutely not. Do they make me a better person in life? They sure do.

You might be thinking, *that's easy for you to say.* But that's because you may not know I was fired from three different companies before we started JPMS, and I was homeless twice. But I'm getting ahead of myself. Just know that when something does not go the way you want in life, be grateful and think about all the things that *did* go right!

Anchors Aweigh

After my high school graduation in 1962, I didn't have the money to go to college, so my next stop was a tour of duty in the U.S. Navy. The Navy was a great experience for me. I joined when I was seventeen years old into the Naval Reserves while I was still in high school. Once I enlisted, I was assigned to the *USS Hornet* aircraft carrier. I traveled to Hawaii and many other places like Japan, Hong Kong, and the Philippines.

In the Navy . . . Robert, Mom, and Me, standing in front of my ship, the USS Hornet

Photos courtesy of author's personal collection

The Navy arranged the very best tours for us; they were only five dollars each, and they included lunch. My brother was with me on the ship for most of those experiences, and we were able to go out there and see the culture and the land on all these tours. We wanted to see the world, and we did. What a great experience!

During my service, I learned management and teamwork skills that were really useful later in my career. I found the Navy to not only be educational and inspirational for me, but it was fun seeing the world. It was one of the best experiences of my life.

I did two years of active-duty military service on the *USS Hornet*. Then two years in the Navy stand-by active duty. I was discharged with honors. All I was hoping for back then was a job that would pay about a hundred fifty dollars a week and let me drive a truck or a car. I've always loved trucks, so getting a job driving a tow truck fit the bill. I could flash my red lights, drive down the wrong side of the freeway, and rescue people. What could be better? After that, I had a bunch of different jobs, including pumping gasoline and selling encyclopedias.

I was fortunate enough to receive the Lone Sailor Award in Washington, D.C. It's an award given to people who were in the military who used some of their experience in civilian life. One of the Admirals suggested I give one or two sentences everybody could remember and take home. I said this: "When I joined the Navy, just like the others, I was just a regular person. However, in the Navy they taught regular people like me how to work together as a team and achieve extraordinary results . . . and that's what I did in civilian life."

Two Keys to Success

Selling Collier's Encyclopedias door to door taught me two valuable lessons for succeeding in business and in life. Without that job, which began in late 1964 soon after my tour in the Navy ended, JPMS might never have happened.

Selling encyclopedias was not easy. It meant showing up at people's homes without an appointment, uninvited and unexpected, in the late afternoon or early evening. Hardly anyone would let an encyclopedia salesman into their homes, and more often than not, they'd close the door in my face. But I became a pretty good encyclopedia salesman. It took time and practice, but I figured it out.

With my briefcase in my hand, I'd knock on the door and say, "Hi, my name is Johnnie D. I'm bringing this new educational program into our area, and I wanted to tell you about it. Do you mind if I step in?"

Slam!

Next door. "Hi, I'm Johnnie D. I've got a new educational program I'm bringing to this area. Do you mind if I step in?"

No, thank you.

Eventually, a door would open, and the person would say, "Yeah, come on in. We'll talk to you a little bit." Finally, those red-and-black-bound volumes came out of my briefcase. "This is the new Collier's Junior Classics," I'd say. "Here's why it's great."

The average encyclopedia salesman lasted about three days back then. I did it for three and a half years and made a pretty good living (even though we were only paid on commission). That experience taught me a lot along the way.

**Colliers' top salesmen before embarking on a
reward trip to Hawaii in 1965. I am 3rd from the right.**
Photo courtesy of author's personal collection.

Lesson number one: Be prepared for rejection. Whether it's a friend, a spouse, a teacher, or a customer, people will reject you . . . and everyone has to face it sometimes. If you're not prepared, rejection can stop you in your tracks. You might think, *Wow, maybe this isn't a good idea, since twenty people said no.* Or, *Hey, they slammed the door in my face ten times. I'm not knocking on another door.* Or even, *No one likes my product, and no one likes me.*

It's not that they didn't like you; maybe they just didn't like the presentation they heard. Being rejected over and over again as an encyclopedia salesman taught me to keep working on my presentation, so the folks behind the next door would be less likely to say no.

To succeed in business or in life, you can't let rejection stop you and you can't take it personally.

Even if twenty, thirty, or a hundred people say "no," you must be able to knock on door #101 with as much enthusiasm as you had before the first hundred doors rejected you. You could have the best product or idea in the world, and you still might get rejected. If you're prepared and you know rejection is coming, you won't stop until you succeed.

If you believe that what you're doing is right, don't give up. I believed everyone needed a Collier's Encyclopedia and every home should have a set. They were easy enough for a high school student to use, and not bad for college kids, either. They may not have been top-of-the-line like Britannica, but everyone needed them. They were easier to read, and there wasn't a doubt in my mind that selling them was the right thing to do. If that meant getting some doors closed in my face, day after day by people who weren't very courteous, then that's the way it would be.

That brings us to: **Lesson number two: The difference between successful people and unsuccessful people is that successful people do all the things that unsuccessful people don't want to do.** My career as an encyclopedia salesman lasted a lot longer than most—not because of any brilliant, natural-born sales ability on my part, but because I was willing to do the things that others didn't want to do. I worked nights and weekends. I was okay with rejection and ready to try again with the next person, knocking on door #101 with a smile on my face and excitement about my product. And never, ever, *ever* giving up.

1991 Reunion in Malibu with fellow Colliers Encyclopedia Sales Management team
L to R: Jerry Friedman, Gene Keesaw, Archie Bakerink, Rex Bakerink, Ross Runnerstrom, Ted Ronnholm, Lou Gross, Don Adams, Me, B.J. Wright, Larry Sovine, and Bill Johnston

From Don Adams

I met JP in California around 1966. We were both selling for Collier's Encyclopedia. The company gave you some education and street smarts, so we thought it was worth it. We'd go into the office every morning at nine o'clock and get driven out to a territory and dropped off around noon. All afternoon, we'd "cold knock" on doors, setting up appointments with housewives and their husbands for later in the day. We'd start with some small talk and eventually come around to showing our product.

Once they were sold on the product, we'd talk about easy ways to purchase it.

I remember one guy who wanted the encyclopedia badly but didn't have the twenty-four dollars and ninety-five cents down-payment to pay for it. Instead, he offered me his 1947 Studebaker that was sitting in the driveway. So, I took it. I'm waiting for my road manager to pick me up and wondering what the hell I was going to do with this car and how I could come up with twenty-four dollars and ninety-five cents to pay for the customer's books, when John comes by. "Hey, Don," he says, "whaddya know? How ya doing?" John Paul was the most enthusiastic guy you ever met. Just a great guy. Everybody liked him. So, I tell him the story and he says, "I need a car for Bella." She was his first wife. Then he gives me thirty-five dollars and, just like that, I got rid of the car. That was John!

Collier's was a positive place to work. Every morning before we went out to knock on doors, we'd spend an hour talking about books like Think and Grow Rich by Napoleon Hill or Dale Carnegie's How to Win Friends and Influence People. And the glass was always half full. There wasn't a single negative word ever spoken. Everything was positive.

There's a story we guys used to preach about an oyster and an eagle. The oyster lays on the bottom of the ocean and never goes anywhere. When he's hungry he just opens his mouth, and the water brings food to him. But the eagle sits on the highest mountain. He fights wind, sleet, hail, and rain and travels hundreds of miles to find food for his family. We all wanted to be eagles so that's what we called ourselves, the Eagles. Since John was a trainer, there were eight offices with Eagles.

Later, I saw John from time to time, after he left Collier's and while he was building his Paul Mitchell business. Then around 1991, we all got together at his beautiful house in Malibu with the hillside view of the ocean. It was like home again with all the guys who worked together when we were young. And we've gotten together since. He may be a billionaire, but John Paul DeJoria has got to be one of the nicest guys I know. He thinks about people and never forgets his old friends. One time at a steak house in Idaho, one of the Eagles told him he was doing a fundraiser for war veterans. John said, "Get a hold of me on Monday. I want to write a check for ten-thousand dollars to give you for their service." You know, it came right out. He was ready to contribute his time and money to them. That's John.

Don't Get Cocky!

Confidence is essential but being overly confident can sometimes lead to disaster. It was 1965, during the Watts riots when it seemed like half of Los Angeles was burning to the ground, and I was still in the encyclopedia business. In my crew was a Black man named Jim, and we were the best of friends. The riots were all over TV. People were shooting and looting stores, when we got the bright idea to head to the middle of the riots to see it for ourselves. We had ignorantly believed that going into a situation of that magnitude—with the idea that we could just go see what's going on and even try to blend in and seem tough—we would be free from danger or consequence. Boy, were we wrong!

I had a rusted old shotgun that my wife's mother had given me. You couldn't shoot that thing if you wanted to, but we put it in the back of the car and drove to 103rd Street and Central Avenue. (I don't know why we thought the idea of having a weapon—even a useless old one—was a good one, but again, we were young and dumb.)

We headed toward downtown LA, pulled over to get some gas, and I put some gas on a towel to clean the window. Then I decided to rub the old shotgun and see if some of the rust would come off before putting it back in the car.

We didn't get a few minutes toward the freeway when suddenly cops were coming from every direction, cutting us off and pointing their guns at my head through the door.

Apparently, someone at the gas station reported seeing two guys with shotguns.

Next thing you know, we're in the L.A. City Jail in a big holding pen with fifty triple-decker bunk beds.

"What are you in here for?" they asked.

Jim quickly says, "Oh, we were harassing cops, we were going down Central Avenue." And the inmates didn't bother us after that, luckily.

Monday morning, we walked into court and the charges were dismissed. We were young, stupid, and behaved without thinking, but we were very lucky to walk away with a valuable life lesson: don't get overly cocky or confident, especially when you're dumb enough to head into trouble.

Homeless the First Time

Sadly, that wasn't my only big mistake during my time as an encyclopedia salesman. My girlfriend and I got married . . . sort of. At nineteen years old, she was one year over the legal age for a woman to get married in Las Vegas, but at twenty, I was a year underage so we used a phony ID. We were just a couple of dumb kids, and it was a crazy thing to do. Then our son came along. After a couple of years, my wife decided she couldn't handle being a mom anymore.

One day, I arrived home and found my wife waiting outside. As I got out of our only car, she climbed in and announced that she was going to the store and that our two-and-a-half-year-old son was waiting in our apartment. Just like that. I went upstairs to our apartment and found John Paul II sitting on the floor, playing with my ripped-up clothes (courtesy of my soon-to-be ex-wife) near a note that said, "I can't take it anymore. He's yours. You're going to fend better than I can. Goodbye." That was it. We didn't see each other again until about five years later.

To make matters even worse, the landlord immediately evicted me. I didn't know my wife hadn't paid the last few months' rent or the electric bills. When she left, she even emptied our bank account taking the little money we had. Suddenly, my son and I were homeless and broke. We literally had nothing, not even a car.

No longer selling encyclopedias, I'd just finished a stint as the master of ceremonies for the second annual Sports, Vacation & Recreational Vehicle Show at the Anaheim Convention Center, but my paycheck wouldn't arrive until the following week. Lucky for me, my wife's mother had an old 1951 Cadillac that she never used. It had a bent-back hood and a leaky water pump that had to be refilled every three or four hours, but this sweet, sweet lady said, "You borrow my car for as long as you need it."

For the next week or so, the back of that car became our home, and our spending money came from returning soft-drink bottles for refunds. In those days, you could get two cents for the little ones and five cents for the big ones at any market or liquor store. People would throw the bottles away or leave them lying next to gas station pop machines or in vacant lots. So, we went around collecting them and turning them in. We also had a little place where we could go and cook. Of course, we could have gone to my mother's house to eat and sleep, but my pride wouldn't let me tell my family or friends how bad off we were.

Each morning, we'd wake up with the sun shining in our eyes and head to nearby Griffith Park, a gigantic city park in the heart of Los Angeles, where we could use the public showers. Then I'd have someone watch my son, while I spent my days trying to hustle up a job. In the meantime, we lived off those soft-drink bottles and counted our blessings. We were lucky to live in America, where every day is a choice. We weren't running from an army or living in a displaced person's camp in some war-torn country. We didn't have to steal from anyone or knock anyone over the head to get what we needed. We could pick up those soft-drink bottles, cash them in, buy a little food, and survive.

Even in those harder times, we had a lot going for us—more than we might have had anywhere else. If you don't give up, things will get better. Looking on the bright side, if you're at the very bottom, the only place to go is up!

Fortunately, it didn't take long to find my next job. It was a sales position, selling dictating equipment for Dictaphone. It certainly wasn't my life's calling, but within a week my first paycheck arrived which was enough money for us to stay at a cheap hotel in a room with a little efficiency stove.

Lee Meyer to the Rescue

One day while I was visiting a friend, my old pal Lee Meyer stopped by. A good friend since junior high, Lee had become a serious biker, complete with tattoos, long hair, and a beard. He rode with friends from a few of the biker dude groups, drinking and getting into more than his share of fights. But he was the salt of the earth and had a huge heart.

"Johnnie, how's it going?" Lee asked. (They still called me Johnnie in those days.)

After hearing what had happened, Lee immediately said, "My mom moved away and I'm living at her house. Why don't you and John Jr. move in with me? The mortgage is forty-seven bucks a month. You pay half and I'll pay half." Twenty-some-odd dollars each . . . it seemed like a miracle. For the second time in my life, Lee Meyer had helped me out.

It wasn't long before Lee's bad-ass but loving community of biker friends became my friends, too. On the weekends, some of those lovely biker ladies and neighbors even watched my son during the day if I had to work. When my son started public school, I'd drop him off during the week, work all day, and then pick him up. That was how we lived for a while.

A Promotion? Forget it

Over the next four or five years, I had an assortment of jobs that helped me polish my sales skills. After working at Dictaphone, I sold photocopiers for Savin Business Machines, printing machines for the AB Dick company, and life insurance for Connecticut General and John Hancock. I even got sales experience from driving a delivery truck for Medico Linen, a company that provided medical supplies and linens to dentists, doctors, and hospitals. Even as a truck driver, I'd try to open new accounts more often than not.

Around 1970, I became circulation manager for Time Inc. in Santa Monica. I ran the renewal circulation department for *Life, Time, Fortune,* and *Sports Illustrated* magazines, where my responsibilities included being in charge of the "boiler room"—fifty people on the phones trying to talk potential customers into subscribing or renewing. The sales pitch included a promise to donate a dollar to the Police Children's Fund. Eventually, when life in the boiler room became excruciatingly dull, I asked my boss, "How do I get promoted?"

"Well, you're just turning twenty-six and you've never been to college," he said. "Come back and ask me when you're thirty-five."

That did it. With no real career path in sight and facing the prospect of ten more years in the boiler room, it became clear to me that having growth and opportunity was very important to me, and I was not willing to give up on achieving it. With that, I decided to explore new job opportunities through the lens of a growth mindset.

I Get Into the Beauty Business

At that time, a man named John Capra worked as an employment counselor, helping individuals find employers to hire them. Today you'd call him an executive recruiter or headhunter. Knowing that my goal was to find a job that had potential, John suggested, "Why don't you take a look at the professional beauty industry?" He knew of a company that was hiring and said, "You won't make much money to start with, but the industry is wide open. It's the beauty industry; you'll have a blast!"

As it turned out, he was absolutely right. It also turned out that I had just met one of my very best friends to this day, fifty-four years and counting.

Me & John Capra

Photo courtesy of author's personal collection

From John Capra

I was a placement agent for a couple of companies when JP first came to my desk in 1969. We just hit it off. I met a lot of salespeople, you know, and many were fast talkers. But John was just a genuinely happy guy. He had a really nice way about him, and I got to know him a little. There was a company called Redken that I knew about because my wife had a beauty shop at the time. I didn't represent them, but I met their salespeople. It was a brand-new type of beauty supply business. They'd go into salons, train hairdressers on different products and help them become better hairdressers by making their clients' hair healthier. I thought it would be a great business for him.

JP was a good-looking guy, had a lot of charisma and a big smile all the time. I knew he was a great salesman from the years he'd spent selling encyclopedias, which was a tough business. JP was a good fit in the hairdressing industry, because he was a fun-loving guy and hairdressers were fun-loving people. Plus, it was great timing. It was the beginning of a new era in the industry that was just taking off. Redken trained him on how to make presentations to hairdressers, and he went on to open up schools and salons for them.

When JP came back from training he called and we got together again. We've been close friends ever since. Meanwhile, he did very well at Redken . . . too well, I guess. The problem was that he didn't fit into the company's mold, so they let him go.

Fired from Three Jobs

My first job in the professional beauty industry was working for Redken Laboratories. It was a great experience and loads of fun. Paula Kent, who was an actress, founded it in 1960 with a hairdresser named Jheri Redding. Redken started with several products and became a leader in the salon product category by the 1970s. In such a rapidly growing environment, it was easy for me to climb the ranks. And I discovered that I loved the business. Just like selling encyclopedias, I learned the features of each product and how they would benefit our customers, then started selling and didn't stop. Combined with a firm belief that our product was the greatest in the world and every salon should have it, my nonstop efforts broke all of Redken's sales records. I learned the basics and applied myself, so it only took me about a year and a half to go from sales rep to national manager of their scientific school and chain salon divisions. My management philosophy was (and still is) to treat people the way I want to be treated.

Unfortunately, the company didn't return the favor. I once walked by a 12' x 12' room with Marmoset monkeys being used for testing. I wanted to take them for a walk, but the scientist said, "No, you can't let them leave the room." So, I went and spoke to the President of the company and the main shareholder and talked about my concern.

I asked, "Guys, why are we doing this? It's not doing any good. We make products for hair, not for skin." Their answer to me was "Because it makes us look good."

A few days later, in 1975, Redken's then Senior Vice President of Sales and Marketing called me in and fired me. He said he had no complaints about my testing methods or annual sales. But my way of running my two divisions—with only two secretaries and four field reps for the whole United States—was making the regional managers look bad. I wouldn't play their animal testing game. I told them it was wrong and had no benefit to hair care products. They said it makes our products look better because it was "Redken, a Scientific Approach." I continually disagreed. Basically, the VP said something like, "In management, you go along with the company's position, even if it's not your own. You need a lot of people to do the work. You're doing the job with too few people. You're doing too much, and you're not about to change. Why don't you get a job selling trucks or jet airplanes and make a good commission? You'll make a fortune. You don't belong in management or running a company or people. We have to let you go."

Around that time, a company called Syntex had purchased the Fermodyl hair product line, and Syntex hired me to train their educational management and sales force on how to sell. In the year I spent with them (1975–1976), their sales revenues went from eight million to twelve million—a fifty percent increase—and then they fired me. I never missed business events, but I didn't hang out with them socially on the weekends. "You're not one of us," they said. Were they serious? At thirty-one years old in the mid 1970s, my idea of a good time was love-ins and not hanging out with the guys on weekends playing cards.

My next stop was the Institute of Trichology, now known as TRI Professional Haircare Products. Founded in the mid 70s by hairstylist Joe Oliveri, they were selling about four-hundred-thousand dollars a year in 1976. They really couldn't afford me, so we struck a deal: my pay would be thirty-six thousand dollars a year plus six percent commission on whatever new growth I produced. After I tripled their sales in the first year, Kent Snow, one of the owners, called me in one day and said, "You made more money than Joe Oliveri did!"

"Well, that's because I gave you a sweetheart deal. You paid me three thousand dollars a month and six percent of all new sales. You got over one hundred percent in new sales, so what's the problem?"

They said, "We have a guy named David Chapman who can do your job for one-third the pay. We have to let you go."

"Why don't you just sell me ten percent of your company?" I suggested. "I'll pay for it over a period of time."

"No, we'll never do that," they said.

Trust in Fate: Life Always Works Out Well

You might think that getting fired from three companies in six years was a bad thing. But after starting JPMS a few years later, I realized something. If I hadn't taken each of those jobs—and got fired from all three—I would *never* have gained the knowledge I needed to start my own company. I'm absolutely convinced that it was heaven-sent. That's the way it was meant to be because something bigger was coming along.

Each of those jobs taught me something valuable about sales, manufacturing, and marketing, which helped me start JPMS. When people fired me for not being their kind of manager, it made me want to be my own manager. When people slammed doors in my face, got bored, or looked away during my presentations, those were educational opportunities to discover what I did wrong. Giving up would not have solved anything; the way to move forward was to just keep going, believing in myself no matter what happened.

Those experiences showed that certain things are meant to be. That's an amazing thing! If you let life take you in the direction you're meant to go, then life works very well. You may not see the benefits right away; sometimes they don't show up until five or ten years later. Everyone's faced with misfortunes in life, but those misfortunes don't define us or stop us unless we let them. How we face our misfortunes and what we learn from our experiences ultimately determines our destiny.

Years ago, I heard a story about the CEO of a major company who walked into the chairman's office and resigned. "I just lost two million dollars," the CEO said. "It's my fault, not anyone else's. Here's my resignation; it's the only thing to do." The wise chairman looked him in the eye, ripped up the resignation, and said, "Are you kidding? I just paid two million for your education, and now you want to leave me?" That chairman recognized the value of turning a negative into a positive. Although it was quite costly, that CEO's mistake could become one of the best learning experiences he'd ever have.

Believe in your mistakes.
God possibly created them as lessons for you.

Chapter 3

Starting a Business with Little to No Money

After the Institute of Trichology fired me, I worked for a couple of years as a consultant for a bunch of different companies. If the client could afford to pay me, I'd tell them everything they needed to know in about three months. Some of the smaller companies needed a lot more than my advice. I'd wind up stepping in and running all their sales and some of their marketing activities. Unfortunately, those companies always seemed to be late in paying me, so that didn't work too well.

— ✻ —

From John Capra

While John was at Redken, he met Paul Mitchell, and they became close buddies. Paul was a genius. Back then, women would go to the salon once a week where they got the usual "bubble" look. Those were the days when they sprayed your hair with concrete, and your hair looked like that until you went back a week later to get it done again. Paul revolutionized hairdressing. He invented cuts and styles that women could recreate at home, using his styling tools and products to continue the look. Before that, beauty stores mainly sold only hairspray!

Paul Mitchell—A Promising Introduction

About a year after I entered the professional beauty industry and during my first year at Redken Laboratories, a mutual friend introduced me to Paul Mitchell. It was 1971 and we were all attending a large industry convention in Florida when salon-chain owner Eva Prang told me, "You have to meet Paul!" Although he was a hairdresser and my focus was sales and marketing, Eva said we shared the same attitudes, and she thought we'd hit it off well. She was right. Over the next nine years, Paul and I became great friends.

Here's a little of Paul's back story. He didn't start off as Paul Mitchell. He was born Cyril Thomson Mitchell in a village in Scotland called Carnwath. His mother and grandmother were hairdressers, the first ones in the village. Following in their footsteps, he trained as a hairdresser in London's West End. He got so good at it that, by the time he was eighteen, he'd won several hairdressing awards and joined a salon in Mayfair. That's when he changed his name from Cyril to Paul. He thought it was a better name.

In the 1960s, Paul joined Vidal Sassoon and became one of London's best-known hair stylists. Then, in 1966, Vidal sent him to the United States where he trained the staff at the first American Vidal Sassoon salon in New York City. Later, Paul opened several Vidal Sassoon salons in New York and introduced something new—the idea of "wash-and-wear" hairstyles. It spread like wildfire throughout the United States. By the time we met in 1971, Paul was a widely respected hairdresser and stylist and a superb platform artist. In the beauty industry, platform artists perform on stage at industry trade shows for hairdressers. They educate hairdressers about new styling techniques and promote the tools or products needed for them. Paul was a rock star on stage.

In 1973, Paul opened his own successful salon (SuperHair) in New York City with Robert Pearson and Robert Clegg. The emphasis was on hair health and cutting, rather than fancy hairstyles. The whole purpose of hair salons was changing back then. Paul was so popular that hairdressers from around the country would show up at his salon to learn about his methods. But Paul was a free soul, and it wasn't long before his edgy thinking got him into big trouble.

In 1974, Paul was boycotted in America by Ralph Evans, who owned *American Hairdresser/Salon Owner* magazine (later *American Salon*). Ralph was also President of the American Beauty Association and the founder, President, and owner of Zotos International. It was a big company and industry pioneer, having launched the first machine-less permanent wave product in 1929, cold waving products in the 1940s, and exothermic and acid waves in the 1970s.

American Hairdresser was founded in 1878 and had a long reputation as the first professional beauty magazine. At the other end of the spectrum was *Viva*, an adult women's magazine that debuted in 1973 and only lasted until 1980. Published by Bob Guccione, editor of *Penthouse*, and his wife Kathy Keeton, *Viva* was a hot, edgy magazine known for its erotic fantasy articles and full-frontal nude photography. The 70s were a wild time, with people "streaking" naked across football fields and the sexual revolution in full swing. Even for those times, Paul was pretty far out there. In August 1974, *Viva* ran a six-page, full-color spread featuring Paul Mitchell's pubic haircuts. His heart, flame, arrow, and wave-shaped haircuts made fashion history. Although many people considered *Viva* cutting-edge, Ralph Evans and the American Beauty Association went ballistic.

Six months later, Paul appeared on the cover of *Viva's* February 1975 edition. In the article titled "Nude News: Macho Hairdressers Undress," Paul was stark naked and covered with tattoos from head to toe, even though he never had a single tattoo (they were all decals, painted, or airbrushed on). That was the last straw. Ralph Evans pulled him out of every hairdressing show and magazine associated with the American Beauty Association and basically, he was blackballed in the United States.

Paul thought it was a good time to sell his New York City salon and move to Hawaii to start over again. He did hair in a one-chair salon in a loft on Bethel Street above a little bar in Honolulu, and he lived in a dinky little house in Waimanalo, with one bedroom and a living room. His "guest room" was parked in the back yard—a little Volkswagen bus with no tires and a mattress in the back. When I visited him there, Paul would stay in the bus and insist that I take the bed. He was a super good guy and a real friend.

You Can't Keep a Good Guy Down

In 1976, my position at Fermodyl gave me the opportunity to bring Paul back to the mainland United States to start doing shows again. Ralph Evans couldn't do a thing about it, because I wasn't a member of the American Beauty Association. They got a little huffy, but Paul came back and his Fermodyl shows were a smashing success. All of a sudden, he was getting back in touch with the industry again. He'd been hosting week-long "Paul Mitchell in Hawaii" seminars until then and, as his popularity returned, we brought him back to the mainland United States more and more often.

In 1979, Paul tried to start a company called PM. He had two shampoos and a conditioner packaged in a white or clear bottle with an orange "PM" on the front. He had no problem selling PM from the stage, but customers weren't reordering. He also paid way too much for making the product, and the quality wasn't as good as it could have been. He'd put a lot of his savings into the company, thinking things would work out, but they hadn't, and he was almost out of money.

After I was fired from Fermodyl and working as a consultant, I offered to consult with Paul as a friend, free of charge, to help reformulate his products and get his business up and running. Although Paul was definitely the king when it came to doing hair, we quickly realized that he didn't know much about running a business. In practically no time, we decided to form a partnership.

From John Capra

A lot of companies back then were testing their products on animals and JP didn't like that at all. He and Paul agreed that there would be no animal testing with the Paul Mitchell products and stuck with it. But other companies made fun of them because of it. I'll never forget one time at a show JP did. These guys ridiculed him. "Who are you going to test your products on," they said, "your grandmother?" They were doing some cruel things with monkeys in those days, like spraying their eyes and doing other things JP was against. Besides having great quality products, he wanted no animal cruelty. He also wanted his products to be safe for the environment. JP was the one to start that movement. The industry might have been ridiculing him but the consumers—and the hairdressers—loved it. JP does the right thing. All his life, he does the right thing. He was very unique in that way and changed the industry.

It was the perfect relationship: I didn't do hair and Paul didn't do the business part, so we had nothing to argue about. Paul would do the hair shows while I ran the business side, including sales, promotion, product development, administration, and just about everything else. We wanted to create a company that offered high quality, professional haircare products at an affordable price through salons and hairdressers. We also wanted to be environmentally correct and not test our products on animals, which many companies were doing. As I look back now, it was probably my experience as an encyclopedia salesman that served me best in those early years. We needed five hundred thousand dollars and finding that money was my job. They'd get forty percent of the company while Paul and I split the rest. We were on our way!

Starting Business with Little to No Money

Counting on the money from the investor, we immediately set everything up so we could hit the ground running when the funds came in.

We enlisted the help of some scientist friends to identify our first three products: a shampoo for normal to color-treated or fine hair, a second shampoo for normal to thick or oily hair, and a leave-in conditioner. Dr. Ron DiSalvo, a world-renowned cosmetic scientist who worked for Redken Laboratories and then consulted for L'Oréal, was kind enough to answer our questions about what we wanted each product to do, such as: "Can you give us an idea of which moisturizer to put in our conditioner so people can leave it in their hair, and it will take care of their scalp, hair, and hands?" (On a side note, Dr. Ron's contributions were so valuable that he eventually became part of our consulting board and our director of research and development. He was a mentor and a friend who worked with us for many, many years.) Bill, who worked at Star Laboratories, was a great resource. He answered questions like, "What are the best ingredients to make our shampoo better than any shampoo on the market today?"

Next, all dressed up in a suit, I visited various vendors and lined up the manufacturers we'd need, including the product formulator, bottle maker, artist, and silk screener.

While visiting the lab that would mix the formula and create the products, my sales pitch went something like, "We're starting a major company and would like to get your pricing. "Calling it a major company at that point was stretching the truth a bit—but we knew that was what it would end up being!

"We'd like to get your pricing for ten thousand pieces, fifty thousand pieces, one hundred thousand pieces, and half a million pieces, to be run in your filling laboratory at one time." Asking for pricing on such large quantities gave the impression that this was a golden opportunity to get in on the ground floor of something huge. Explaining what we wanted the product to do, I'd say, "If you'll work with me on this, I'll give you our business." It worked.

By the time I met with the bottle maker, my excitement had really grown, so I skipped the pricing for ten thousand pieces and went straight to the top: "How much would it cost for fifty thousand, one hundred thousand, a quarter of a million, and half a million pieces?"

With product and bottle pricing in hand, my next stop was the silk screener, who would put the labels on each bottle. "What does it cost for a hundred thousand, a quarter million pieces?" I was over the moon by now.

I was so excited! We had half a million dollars coming in, and we were starting our company.

By February 1980, we had our first three products ready to show off and were getting set to launch the company. We had our backer and half a million dollars was arriving that day from our investor. Money was coming from Jersey, one of the Channel Islands between England and France. Paul flew in to celebrate. We were so excited. The gods were behind us. Everything was going our way.

We didn't see it coming.

A Fateful Call

The big day arrived and . . . nothing. We waited all day and night. The money wasn't there. We looked at each other and said, "What do we do?" It was three o'clock in the morning in England, long after the banks had closed. I called Dick Holthouse, a vice president of Citicorp Europe at the time, and he gave me the bad news: "I hate to tell you this," he said, "but the backer changed his mind." It was early 1980. Inflation was at twelve and half percent, unemployment at ten and a half percent, prime interest rates at seventeen percent, and everyone waited in line to get gas. Our backer didn't want to take a risk.

What a day that was! If losing five hundred thousand dollars wasn't bad enough, that was also the day my second marriage ended. Things hadn't been going well between us, so I settled my wife and daughter, Alexis, into our house, with a nice car, all the bills paid, and several thousand dollars to tide them over for the next few months. I left with a few hundred dollars in my pocket, and my twenty-year-old car. Saying goodbye to my old life of instability, I was ready for a new chapter that would provide security and consistency for my family, With this mindset, I headed to the bank to meet Paul.

Since we had believed the startup money was coming in that day, I figured I'd stay in an inexpensive hotel room until I found an efficiency apartment. I wasn't worried because we had a great business partnership and a great future ahead of us. Paul was running out of money, too, so we were pretty eager to get that five hundred thousand dollars. Instead, that shocking phone call left both of us broke and me homeless for the second time in my life.

Paul cash reserves were dwindling, but he had a place to live. I had a few hundred bucks and my car to sleep in. We needed money and needed it fast. Paul said, "I don't have a lot, but I can spare three-hundred and fifty dollars." I went to my mom but didn't want to tell her how bad things were. She thought my family was doing well; she knew we had a nice home on Mulholland Drive. She had no idea that I'd just moved out, and was living in my car for the second time in my life. I just said I was short on cash and asked to borrow a few hundred bucks.

"Oh sure, Son," she said. "Everything okay?"

"Yeah, it's fine."

Between Paul's three-hundred and fifty dollars, the little money I had, and the loan from my mom, we had seven hundred bucks between us and a few hundred for me to live off. But we thought we were lucky. Crazy, right? We believed in ourselves and knew we could do anything if we put our minds to it. Well, the feeling was there anyway, so we just said, "What the hell, let's just go for it!" And we put everything on the line.

So, here's what happened.

First, I called the bottle man, a little humbler now, and said, "I'd like to have a sample order of only ten thousand bottles. Could you please ship them to the silk screener?" Praying, praying, *Please do it, please do it.*

"Sure," he said, "and we'll give you thirty-day billing!"

Oh my goodness, we got the bottles! I did the same thing with the lab that was mixing the formulas, and they agreed as well.

When it came time to call the silk screener, I crossed my fingers, mustered as much confidence in my voice as I could, and said, "We have a sample run of ten thousand bottles coming. Would you please screen three thousand Shampoo One, three thousand Shampoo Two, and four thousand bottles of The Conditioner?" He agreed!

"We have thirty-day billing set up with the laboratory," I said. Would it be okay if you gave us thirty-day billing, too?"

"Sure," the silk screener said again. "The lab gave you thirty? Thirty's wonderful."

Since color ink was too expensive, we settled on a black-and-white logo. We didn't realize it at the time, but that was actually a stroke of luck. Our unisex black and white design appealed to both men and women, and it turned out to be timeless.

The only vendor who wouldn't agree was the artwork designer. He wanted a thousand dollars up front and wouldn't budge on his terms. We tried everything to get him to change his mind. "We'll pay you in thirty days," we said, but he turned us down flat. So, we got honest.

If Everything Else Fails, Be Honest

Scamming and bluffing might work some of the time, but when it comes to getting things done, dishonesty will only wreck you in the long run. Honesty always pays.

"Look man, here's the scene," we said. "We have the bottles and everything else lined up, but our investor pulled out. We only have seven hundred dollars. That's it! Can we pay you three or four hundred now and give you the rest later?"

The artist said, "I hate to be a bad guy, but I'll take the seven hundred dollars. It's three hundred less than I want, but I know I'll never see the rest." So, we paid him the seven hundred bucks. Now we were really broke.

Living in L.A. on $2.50 a Day

Since the bottle manufacturer and silk screener had agreed to a thirty-day credit line, we had a little wiggle room. We figured it would take about two weeks for the bottles to leave the manufacturer, go to the silk screener, and then go to the filling company for product to be added. That left us two weeks to make some sales before the bills were due. In the meantime, we'd have to scrape by somehow.

It's amazing how resourceful you can be when you need to be. In those first two weeks after our backer fell through, my house was once again my car. I remembered from my earlier homeless days that city parks often had free showers. The Griffith Park tennis courts became my home away from home. Boy, did I love that place! It was clean, it was convenient, and best of all, it was free. And a lot of people left their soap or shampoo behind, so I had it made.

Eating was a bigger challenge but, with a little creativity, it was possible to get by on two dollars and fifty cents a day. Most big cities (and even some smaller ones) have truck stops near the highways and freeways, and most of them offer a breakfast special. For ninety-nine cents, the Freeway Café truck stop served one egg, one piece of toast, a few pieces of potato, a strip of bacon or sausage (or ham), and a cup of coffee or juice. I could take care of both breakfast and lunch if I stopped there around ten o'clock in the morning, ordered the special, and ate every last bite – along with the jam, the ketchup, and every scrap on my plate. It was like a midmorning brunch.

What about dinner? A big-chain restaurant, El Torito, was the first to start a "happy hour" from 4:30 to 6pm. They offered ninety-nine-cent drinks and all-you-can-eat appetizers. Drinks were usually the cheap stuff. By heading there in the late afternoons, dinner was early enough and filling enough to satisfy the afternoon munchies and get me through the night.

You'd be surprised at how full you can get on ten or so chicken wings, mini tostadas, and a whole lot of salsa! It was like a full meal. It left me feeling pretty good and I had a fairly well-balanced diet.

Leaving a good tip turned out to be important at happy hour. "I'm down and out, but look," I'd say, "I'm buying a drink for ninety-nine cents and giving you a twenty-five percent tip. Here's twenty-five cents." After a few nights they caught on and I told them I was down and out and trying to start a new company. The waitress said, "God bless you, you're going in the right direction here," and she'd hand me a few more tortillas or a little something extra on the side. They didn't have to, and I didn't need it to exist, but it was a nice thing to do and I appreciated it more than they'll ever know. When I finally made some extra money, I went back and gave them each a very big tip.

Even on my two-dollar and fifty-cent budget, I had enough to eat and a little left over for gas money. I parked my car on Mulholland Drive because it was safe there.

That's how I got through those first two weeks, until a young actress named Joanna Pettet knocked on my car window one day. Joanna had appeared in the TV series *Dr. Kildare* and would later appear in *Knots Landing.* We knew each other from years past. "I heard you were living in your car," Joanna said. "I have a room in my house I could loan you for a couple of months at no rent. Come on, no strings attached, man. Let me give you a helping hand."

The room was free if I wanted it for the first two months, and after that I'd have to pay rent. What a wonderful lady!

Fake It 'til You Make It

Now that I had a place to live, I had an office, too. Well, that might be a slight exaggeration since my office consisted of a twenty-nine dollar and ninety-five cent answering machine and a sixteen-dollar-a-year post office box at the Universal City post office. We had business cards printed with "John Paul Mitchell Systems, P.O. Box 8625, Universal City, CA" along with our phone number. When someone called, they'd hear the lovely English accent of my friend Caroline on the answering machine saying, "Helllooooo, John Paul Mitchell Systems. I'm terribly sorry but we're all out right now. Things are really booming! If you'll leave a message, we'll call you back when we return." Suddenly our little company sounded much bigger than it was. No one ever guessed it was just Paul, a nonexistent secretary, and me.

We also needed stationery, and since our funds were tight it would have to be homemade. This was before computers became mainstream, so I wrote up our letterhead and took it to a print shop. For an extra five dollars and fifty cents they typeset it, made a copy, and handed it back to me. Then I went and made photocopies. Click, click, boom—we had stationery!

From there, it was easy to create invoices for the orders that we hoped would start pouring in any time. Using a sheet of stationery, I'd write the name of the products on one side, the individual price in the middle, and the total at the end. It's always amazing how much you can do when you put your mind to it.

One of the biggest challenges in those first few weeks was sleeping in my car and still managing to put on a jacket and my best poker face to sell our new business without letting anyone know we were really down and out. It was tough but I firmly believed that what we were doing was worth it.

From John Capra

I didn't know he was living in his car back then. Do you think I would allow him to live in his car if I'd known? At the time, we had just adopted children, and he knew the difficulties we'd had, trying to have children. He'd come to our house, bringing me a gift, and telling me how happy he was for me. He talks about you, not him. That's how he is. He just doesn't bring those things to you. He wants you not to be concerned about him. Are you okay? he'll ask. That's always been his MO (modus operandi).

There But for Me Go I

If there was one thing life had shown me over and over again, it's that with time and focus, things always get better. My mom had proven it as she worked hard and saved every dime to buy our very own home. And my own experiences proved it, too. As a kid learning gymnastics, I could barely get on the pommel horse at first. Then all of a sudden, I could flip my leg over it. Then I could flip my whole body over it. After a while, I was doing scissors and spins. With practice and focus, it's amazing how much better you get.

At Collier's Encyclopedia, my manager, BJ Wright, was a successful young man, about twenty-eight years old. Like most successful people, he did a lot of things that other people didn't want to do. For example, he didn't have to work on Saturdays but he'd come into the office anyway, do his work, and then go empty his own trashcan. Since no one else came in on Saturdays, BJ would show up unshaven, wearing cut-up jeans and tie-dyed T-shirts (the style in 1966).

He certainly didn't look like the regional manager of Collier's Encyclopedia, and he didn't look like someone earning a hundred-fifty thousand dollars a year (the equivalent of more than one and a half million in 2025).

BJ's office at the corner of Spring and Seventh Streets in Los Angeles was about two blocks away from Skid Row. The office trash bins were located in an alley behind the building, right near the Mayfair Hotel restaurant. In those days, homeless folks from the Skid Row mission would come to the alley and dig through the restaurant trash in hopes of finding some food.

One Saturday, BJ was dumping the trash as he always did, when a drunken man came down the alley toward him, singing loudly as he staggered along and smelling of cheap wine or Sterno. Although he was clearly destitute, he walked up behind BJ and said, "Sir, you don't have to look in that trashcan to get food." Thinking that BJ was hungry and searching for food, the man pulled a dime from his pocket and said, "Sir, take this dime, go to the donut shop, and get a donut and a cup of coffee on me."

BJ, one of the most successful young men of the day, was flabbergasted as he watched the man barely make it down the alley. *Wait a minute,* BJ thought. *This guy's generous, just like I am. He's smiling. He's enthusiastic, and even though he's drunk, he seems happy giving.*

BJ thought, This must be some message from God. This guy's too much like me, but he's destitute and I'm not. What's the message? It has to be something big.

BJ went back to his office and spent the whole morning writing and writing, thinking and thinking. When he was done, he came up with one sentence. That powerful sentence was this: There but for me go I.

You see, BJ Wright came from a poor family in Kentucky. If it wasn't for the choices he made in his life, he could have ended up exactly like that destitute man. "There but for me go I."

When you stop to think about it, the drunkard could have reached the same conclusion. He was a lot like BJ Wright. If he had decided to make different choices and take a different course in life, could he have become successful, too?

We all make decisions in life. Sometimes they're good, sometimes not so good.

By the way, a few decades ago, BJ and I reconnected and continue to see each other about once a year. He started a successful water purification company that became a family business, now managed by his son and daughter since BJ retired.

Those "overnight success" stories you sometimes hear rarely happen overnight. They usually come after years of someone rolling up their sleeves, working hard, and making sacrifices.

Chapter 4
Strategies for Sales Success

Two weeks after ordering the first batch of bottles, we had the product in our hands, as we had hoped. Now it was time to start selling so we could pay those bills!

For the next two weeks, Paul worked salons in Hawaii, giving free demonstrations to stir up interest and create buzz while I tapped into my previous experience as a door-to-door encyclopedia salesman. Filling my car with shampoo and conditioner, I pounded the pavement, trying to sell our three original products directly to beauty salons.

At each salon, I'd ask to see the owner to demonstrate the features and benefits of each product before asking if they'd like to try "only a dozen" of each. They'd say something like, "Well, no, not really. It's a new product. Come back some other time."

My stock reply was, "I'm convinced you'll love this new product. If you'll agree to take just six bottles each of Shampoo One, Shampoo Two, and The Conditioner, and you're not totally happy, I'll come back in a month and give you your money back for any bottle you haven't used or sold." I'd look them in the eyes and, nodding my head, add, "Now, that's fair enough, isn't it?" Two months later, when we added our new Sculpting Lotion, I'd say, "Let me hold a quick meeting with your staff on how to use it. I know you'll be happy."

Being as honest and helpful as possible and giving people a reason to buy sometimes did the trick; they'd hand me the money or write me a check.

Of course, not every salon said yes. Maybe one out of every five agreed, while the other four said, "No" or "Come back later."

When twelve salons finally agreed to buy from me, I went to Jim Henrietta, President of Paris Ace Beauty Supply in Los Angeles, and asked, "How would you like to be the distributor for the new Paul Mitchell line?"

Jim said something along the lines of, "I carry all these really big lines. Why would I want your little line?" (Helene Curtis®, Redken®, Matrix®, Jhirmack®, and Revlon® were the major manufacturers at that time.)

Handing him my orders and checks, I said, "Because I have your first twelve customers right here!"

"Wow, that's pretty good," Jim said.

"And I'll ride around with your salespeople and help them sell this product."

At that time in the professional beauty products industry, it was standard procedure for manufacturers to give their distributors a discount. We couldn't afford to mark down our products, so we built the discount into our pricing and told the distributors that if they paid their bills when the products were delivered, we would give them a five percent discount. In other words, if we wanted to sell for a dollar, we priced the product at one dollar and five cents. Over the course of a year, the distributor would get a pretty good discount, and we could collect the money quickly—which we needed to do because we had no money.

"The only thing I ask from you is the check when the products are delivered," I told Jim. "If you buy two-thousand dollars worth of my products and give me a check right now, I'll give you an extra five percent discount. Even better, if you buy two-thousand dollars from us, you can also be our exclusive distributor for greater Los Angeles and Orange County."

"We're Paris Ace Beauty Supply. We don't pay our bills for forty-five days," he said.

It was time to get brutally honest again: "But we really need the money."

Jim laughed and said, "Okay, I'll give you a break this time, but only if you show up when the products arrive and work with my salesman."

Of course, I agreed—then went straight to my car to deliver the product to the warehouse.

Five minutes later, the warehouse makes a call. "Jim, there's some guy back here unloading a product and he wants the check."

I could hear Jim laughing and happily yelling through the phone, "He was just in my office!"

He came back with a check. Thank you, Jim, for helping me start John Paul Mitchell Systems.

You Can Do It: Here is Some Help

Talking to people was never a problem for me, so selling always came easily. When I was four years old, my mother took my brother and me to a small Christian camp in Little Green Valley, near Lake Arrowhead and Crestline in southern California. We stayed in a little log cabin and on Sunday morning everyone gathered together, sitting on log benches while the preacher told a few stories. No one knows what moved me to do this, but during one of those sessions I stood up, walked over to the preacher, and said, "I want to tell a story." My mom's mouth dropped, and so did the mouths of the two or three dozen other people there. No doubt, they were all wondering, *What's this kid going to do?*

Standing straight and tall, I told them a Bible story I remembered from Sunday school. At the end, my mom said with amazement in her eyes, "What a surprise! That was very good, Johnnie." I sat down, thinking nothing of it, like it was just one of those things that happened all the time.

If you're thinking, *I could never do that. I don't have the confidence to walk up to someone and start talking*, please know that talking to people and selling a product are easier than you think, if you follow these few sales tips. You may or may not find them in a textbook on sales, but they worked when our company was getting started and I'd love to share them with you.

Know the Features and Benefits

When we started JPMS, we had no money for advertising (remember, we were broke), so we decided to sell through education. It was a unique approach; as far as we knew, no other company had done it before. We sold our products by focusing on two keywords: *features and benefits.*

Whatever your product may be, tell people about its features and how it will benefit them. For example, a seamstress might say, "I can alter clothes better than anyone's ever altered clothes for you," or "I can sew stuff together better than anyone ever has." That's the feature: *I can sew better than anybody else. The benefit is: The clothes I'm going to make for you will look tailor-made and three or four times more expensive than they really are.*

Let's say you're starting a window washing service. You might say, "I'm the best window washer in the world. I don't just whip through your window; I start in the upper corner, go straight down, and clean every inch. I clean inside and outside until it's perfect, and that's why I'm the best there is. No one else will wash your windows as well as I will. And by the way, when I'm done, your whole building will look a lot better because of what I did and the care I take." Always give people the features and benefits.

When we started the company, one of our benefits was a money back guarantee for any product that didn't sell. In our first ten years of doing business that way, we only had one bottle ever returned—and it was ninety percent empty!

Present Your Product, Don't Show It

If you're showing someone your product (or even if you're only showing them a flyer describing your product or services), hold it with pride, as if it were a million-dollar bill or a valuable gem. To add value to our early product sales, I went to a fabric remnant shop and spent a dollar for one perfectly cut square foot of purple velvet material. At each salon, I'd carefully set my piece of velvet down and place my products on top of it, to create the best presentation I possibly could. Love your product or service.

Speak with Conviction

When you talk to someone, look them right in the eye. If that feels too uncomfortable, then look them right between the eyes. Or you could look at their eyebrows. Sounds silly but it really works! You'll look like you're looking them in the eye.

If you look away while you're talking to someone, they feel like they don't have your full attention. If you're talking and the person looks away, stop talking; they'll look right back at you because they'll feel uncomfortable. You must have people's full attention to communicate with them.

When you ask a question such as, "Do you want to buy?" customers want to feel your sincerity. Look them in the eye, nod your head, and ask, "That would be okay, wouldn't it?" If they say, "Well, I don't know," give them an either/or option such as, "I can appreciate that. Perhaps you're more comfortable with only one of each? Which would you prefer?" Instead of yes or no, give them another option and they'll be more likely to choose one or the other.

One Speaker at a Time

If you're having a conversation and the other person starts talking before you're done, don't say another word. If you keep rambling while they're chiming in, they won't hear a word you say. It's a fact: when someone's talking, they can't hear anyone else. Wait until they're done. Listen to them, if you can. Don't worry—you won't lose your place. You know what you're going to say, so listen quietly and when they're done, you'll have your turn to say your part. It's the nice thing to do.

Three Timeless Success Strategies

The success of those early sales came down to three key concepts that continue to guide JPMS to this day. In developing our products, we identified a need and filled it, we created a top-quality product, and—from day one—we've been loyal to our customers who, in return, are loyal to us.

#1: Find a Need and Fill It

Most people who've been to a beauty salon can tell you that their hair looks wonderful when they walk out the door, but two or three days later it doesn't look the same. Wouldn't it be great if they could figure out how to make that hairstyle look the same between their monthly or bimonthly visits? When we developed our first Paul Mitchell products, we identified that need and filled it: Our goal was to help people keep their hair looking better between salon visits. Our leave-in conditioner improved blow-dry results for salon looks both in the salon and at home.

When we asked ourselves what other needs our products could fill, one of the answers was "more time in the stylist's day." By creating a single-application shampoo (no more "lather, rinse, repeat"), we shaved ten minutes from the shampoo process. Our leave-in conditioner meant no time to "wait and rinse."

We saw the needs in the marketplace and filled them with our products.

#2: Produce a Quality Product

One of the most important keys to business success is having the *highest quality products and/or services* in your category. From day one, we did not want to be in the *selling* business; we wanted to be in *the reorder business*, by making a top-quality product that people would want to buy over and over again. How many hair care products can you name that are manufactured the same way more than four decades later and still selling? Our earliest products—Shampoo One, Shampoo Two, The Conditioner, Sculpting Lotion, and Freeze and Shine—all are still great sellers after forty-five years because the products were that good. A great product or service can become timeless.

#3: Be Loyal to Your Customers

Our product was hair care, and we decided to sell only through or somehow benefit the professional salon industry. Hairstylists would use our products, see how good they were, and recommend them to their customers to make their hair look its best between salon visits. We firmly believed and continue to believe that hairdressers know which products will work best to create their clients' hairstyles. We also promised the beauty industry that if they'd support us and buy our products, we'd continue to benefit the professional beauty industry: we would be loyal to our customers. I cemented that promise in 2004 by creating a 360-year trust that gives my directive for JPMS to remain a privately owned, independent company that will benefit our good salons no matter how buying or distribution habits change.

Leave It at the River

Despite our best efforts in those first two weeks, when the thirty-day deadline rolled around, we didn't have enough money to pay the bill. We dragged out the old standard line and told our creditors, "The check is in the mail" or "I'll drop it off." Two days later, we had just enough to cover that debt, but it was a full two years before we could finally pay our bills on time. Until then, every week was, "The check is being mailed; the check will be coming, please don't cut us off." Or "I'll hand deliver it the day after tomorrow." It was miserable.

I was so worried about not being able to pay the bills that I often couldn't sleep at night.

Did lying awake and worrying about paying the bills help me?

Absolutely not!

**Academy Award winner, my friend James Colburn, and Me;
We shared a love of riding motorcycles**
Photo courtesy of author's personal collection

My good friend, James Colburn, an Academy Award -winning actor and incredible guy, once told me a story about letting go of the past and moving forward in the present. It showed how you can't change "yesterday's news", but you can find ways to put it behind you.

It seems that two Buddhist monks were on a pilgrimage when they came to a fast-flowing river. A beautiful young lady was standing nearby, afraid to cross to the other side. The elder monk walked over, picked her up, carried her across the river, and set her down. The younger monk followed behind and the pair continued their journey. That night at their campfire, the younger monk said, "Sir, I have a question to ask. It's been on my mind all day long. We vow never to touch a woman, yet you picked up this beautiful girl, put her in your arms, and walked across the river. Why did you do that?" The elder monk simply replied, "I left her at the river this morning, but you've been carrying her around all day long. Leave it at the river!"

Here's one other strategy for letting go of worries. If something bothers you, try writing it down on a piece of paper. Read it over and keep writing until you capture everything that worries you, and you see it in its entirety. An amazing thing can happen: you might find that you don't care anymore. Just like the senior monk, you don't have to carry it anymore, because it's on that piece of paper. You can put it in a drawer and look at it the next day or next month, next year, or whenever you want. It's out of your mind, but it's there if you need it. Chances are, you won't need it, though. You can leave it by the river.

Chapter 5

Doing More With Fewer Moving Parts

For our first year in business, Paul and I lived on people's couches, took buses and midnight flights when we traveled, and ran the company from wherever I was because we had virtually no money. We ran it using the telephone and taking credit cards.

Paul's job was to sell our Paul Mitchell products through trade shows with hairdressers. About three months in, Jeanne Braa, a stylist Paul had worked with in Hawaii, became his stage partner, helping him by using our products and demonstrating the results. Together they taught the latest hairstyling techniques and showed salon professionals how to use Paul Mitchell products. At the start, she did it for expenses only, then continued to work with Paul for the next nine years until his death. She was a wonderful and talented lady as well as the first Artistic Director at JPMS.

From Jeanne Braa Foster

I met Paul when we were both living in Hawaii around 1978. I'd heard that this guy was "it!" He was doing perms at the time because fashion has everything to do with product and being ahead of the curve. I was a good perm wrapper, which I'd learned from my grandma, and I started wrapping perms for him like hotcakes. He was impressed. With Paul's help, I got a job at the best salon in town, but I still had to build up a clientele. Every night I'd go out soliciting clients—girls who worked as bartenders and in clothing and department stores—and offered them first-time, free haircuts. By three months I had more clients than hairdressers who'd been there for three years! Paul was super impressed and invited me to assist him in a hair show. I loved it.

In the meantime, Paul and JP were putting together their business plan. Paul invited me to LA to meet JP, who was living out of his car at the time. His trunk was full of his clothes, but everything was pressed and beautiful. So, Paul was the cutting edge, out-of-the-box, hair-cutting star and JP was the marketing genius, the man who could sell anything to anybody. Both of them loved their moms and did a lot to help them, so they had that in common. Together they were hungry, hungry, hungry. So was I.

This was how we started doing hair shows. JP would go to a city and find someone who'd buy enough product to bring Paul and me in. If they met his quota, he'd tell them they could be a distributor and sell the product at the hair show. Then Paul and I would come and do the show, which would be in a small hotel ballroom. Meanwhile, JP would go to the next town and sell enough product to get us there. It's how he built our distributor network. JP has made more millionaires than anybody I know. He's a millionaire maker, because he knows the people who are hungry.

Sometimes, Paul would go ahead with JP and leave me behind. I would help follow up by visiting salons and educating hairdressers. Here's the crazy thing. Most of the people who brought us in kept us at their houses and fed us! They'd host us like missionaries, and we'd make friends with them. If we had to stay in a hotel and feed ourselves, we'd always go to a nice place and eat appetizers instead of entrees. Paul was not a fast-food guy. And he always said a prayer before every meal.

Before every show, we always had a glass of champagne. Because it was a party. It was fun. We weren't there to teach and sell. We were there to build people up, make them want to love what they do and please their clients. If their client only looks good when they leave the salon, it's not good for business. But if their client looks good all the time, it makes them look good. We were there to build up the hairdressers, which built up the distributor. So, you always start with the hairdresser.

We always brought something new over the years, something ahead of its time. That was the challenge. Paul would find ways to cut that were out-of-the-box. We wanted our hairdressers to always learn something new. We wanted them to have fun. We would do two to four shows a week. If people got too serious, we'd say, "It's not brain surgery. It's just a hair show." Our rooms were always fun and happy.

The best thing about working with JP and Paul was more than their amazing product. It was never just business for JP. It was a cause. And that cause was building up people. He would hire people that weren't super qualified, groom them, and build them up. Everyone connected with JP knew it was a cause, a family. When JP introduced you, it made you feel like a million dollars.

When Paul passed, I chose to stay with JP. He just took hold of the baton and stepped into the role. There was no one who could replace Paul, but JP had a way of holding everybody together on the business side. We created a team of innovative, talented stylists and called them the core group. And it was still fun. I was on the board, and we held our board meetings on the beach in the early days. I trusted JP so much, right from the start. He always took care of everybody. He was like a brother to me. Although I've moved on since, I still love JP. I respect and thank him for giving me the life I had.

Getting Through the First Two Years

Six months after we started, we hired our first employee; her name was Shirley Wong. Working out of my house, Shirley took on everything I'd been snowballed with. She answered the phone instead of me checking the answering machine after I got home. She handled the mail, kept the books, sent the invoices, and picked up the merchandise. She wore so many hats: receptionist, order taker, order processor, accountant, bill collector, and just about every role anyone could hold in an office.

A year and a half into the journey, we hired our second employee. Paul was still selling at trade shows, I called on salons, and Robert Stafford became the third member of our sales force, working with distributors and their salespeople in the field, teaching them how to use and sell the products when they called on salons.

It was two hard years before we could pay our bills on time; we didn't pay them off, but we managed to pay them on time. In our first year, we did a little over four-hundred and forty-thousand dollars in business. In the second year, we hit 1.3 million dollars. With no loans and most of our income invested in inventory, that left just enough profit to give ourselves two-thousand dollars each. We were on top of the world and felt like we'd finally made it!

In all honesty, every week for almost two years we should have gone out of business. Any business textbook would have told us, "Guys! Go bankrupt, go bankrupt! There's no hope for you. You can't even pay your bills on time." But our attitude, ingenuity, and the help of a lot of people along the way kept us going and led to success no one in those early days would have imagined.

Never, Never, Never Give Up

About five months into the business, a fellow named Gerald Koch wanted to be our distributor in Georgia. He hadn't hired any salespeople yet but we were both good salesmen (or so we thought), so I shipped some product to Georgia and we decided to call on Atlanta salons together.

With just the two of us in the field, we set a goal for the day: to sell five hundred dollars' worth of Paul Mitchell products into salons that had never heard of us before. By noon, we had sold only forty-seven dollars' worth. One bottle here, another there. We were not off to a very good start.

It was very hot, in the middle of summer, so we headed to a pizza place. Gerald ordered a nice, cold beer and I decided to have one, too. About halfway through eating our pizza we realized, "What are we doing? This beer is going to slow us down!" We stopped drinking, finished our pizza, and said,

"We're going to do this." By 6:30 that night, we reached our five-hundred-dollar goal.

There was no sudden "aha" or change to our strategy. We did the same things that afternoon that we'd done earlier in the day. We just kept going and never gave up. It's a lot like horse racing: the horse that starts in the back of the pack doesn't always lose. If you start slow, then pick up momentum, and suddenly you have it. We worked like that horse in the back of the pack—we just kept going.

In sales and in life, we often get rejections and challenges along the way. Remember what I said earlier: successful people are just as enthusiastic after door number fifty is slammed in their face as they were at door number one. I can never say it enough.

Successful people prepare for rejection. They never give up.

Maybe we just got our punches that morning, but even if our luck had not turned around that afternoon and we sold nothing at all, we would have headed out with the same excitement on the following day. Is it really that easy? *No! It was hard.* But you have to keep going if you want to succeed.

Doing More With Fewer Moving Parts

Being broke and learning how to run a lean business taught us another powerful lesson: if you give people the chance to expand their own abilities, they'll rise to the challenge. When we hired Shirley Wong, we needed someone who could take over my ten jobs and free me up to run the company and spend more time in the field. Shirley was not only capable, she was excited to take on the challenge. She was a real visionary.

Most employees are tasked with just one job so that's all they ever do. Over time, they could probably do that job in half the time, but since they're never challenged, they'll spend the whole day on that one job. We learned that giving people more responsibility, paying them well, and giving them credit when they get the job done gives them a chance to be great. They just need the opportunity and the chance to grow.

In the first couple of years, we didn't have the money to afford a warehouse of our own. We had to be careful about shipping costs. So, I'd drive to the lab that manufactured our products, load up my car, and make in-person deliveries. We shipped Paul's orders to Hawaii, and he made his own deliveries, too. When we signed with a distributor and increased our sales, we made a deal with the lab: we would contribute to their warehouse worker's salary—a gentleman named Angel—and they'd ship our products to distributors. Angel unofficially worked for us part time, getting our shipments out. When we eventually got our own warehouse, we brought him onboard, and he still works with us after forty-plus years!

We started the practice of "fewer moving parts" through necessity, and it has been our business philosophy ever since.

Treat People the Way You Want to Be Treated

Another practice that got us through those first few years was building strong relationships with hairdressers and distributors. We could have the best product in the world, but nothing is more important than the people we work with and the people we serve. They're more important than anything else and they deserve our attention and our time.

Rule #1: The customer is always right.

Rule #2: Even if they're wrong, they're still right. Do something to please them. Get your ego out of it or you won't have any clients.

Because of our loyalty and gratitude for their business—especially for taking a chance on a small, new company—we promised from the very beginning that we would only sell Paul Mitchell products in a way that would somehow benefit our professional beauty salons. Other companies had made that promise and reneged, but we intended to honor our word.

In those days, distributors typically carried twenty to fifty different product lines. Our job was to get them to like us and help them have success with our products so they'd be willing to introduce them to their customers. It wasn't always easy. Our first distributor was a fellow in Texas who took us on but dropped us two months later, saying, "Guys, this is going nowhere. You only have three products." Thankfully, we had a solid background in accepting rejection and just kept knocking on those doors!

Selling Through Education

Our third strength in the early years was teaching stylists and distributors how to use and sell our products for take-home use. Since we had no money for advertising, we needed a different way to engage prospective buyers. We did it through education. We offered salons a money-back guarantee if they'd let us show their staff how to use and sell the products.

"If you agree to buy a dozen each (we'd actually start at three dozen each and work our way down to a dozen if needed), put it on your shelf, and display it at eye level, we will come in and show your staff how to use and recommend it with this guarantee: if in one month it's not the finest, hottest product line you've ever used, we'll take back every bottle you haven't used or sold and give you your money back. Now, that's fair enough, isn't it?"

Once they agreed, we'd return with the product and hold a clinic for their salon team. We'd show them how to hold the bottle, how to put The Conditioner in the client's hand and tell them how to use it, and how to talk about it while putting it in their hair. (Here's a fun little sales tip: you have a captive audience when you put something in the customer's hand.)

As our company grew and we began working with more distributors and their salespeople, and eventually with our own sales force, we taught them that exact process. I would spend a day in the field with a sales trainee, making sales calls. First, the trainee would watch and listen to my presentation. Afterwards, I'd review what I'd said and why I'd said it. After half the day, the trainee would give it a try. By the end of the day, the trainee's presentation was just like mine and ready to go.

During our second year in business, we started what we called our Associate program for hair stylists who wanted to be platform artists. Training in salon classes helped get them comfortable talking in front of crowds and doing in-salon presentations. When ready, many of them joined us on stage in shows. As our company grew, people were honored and proud to be called Paul Mitchell Associates.

The Ultimate High

At the end of that second year, with all the bills paid on time and two thousand dollars for each of us, we were so excited. It was a turning point for me with JPMS, and I'll never forget it. We looked at each other and said, "Hey, you know, we made it!" We knew it was going to be great from here on in. Two thousand dollars may not seem like a lot of money today, but it was for me back in 1982.

That called for a celebration! A friend and I went down to the El Torito restaurant in Marina del Rey and, for the first time in my life, I ordered from the left side of the menu. You know . . . the side that tells you what you get, not the side that tells you how much it costs. Usually, going someplace with very little money, I'd go through the how-much-does-that-cost and what-can-I-get-for-it routine. But on this amazing day, things were different.

The most expensive thing on the menu was carne asada for about ten bucks, and a big margarita was about two bucks (they didn't have Patrón tequila yet, but that was okay). We could have anything we wanted, and order from the left side of the menu.

Sitting right in front of us was a table with about twelve kids and a mom at each end, and they looked like they were from the inner city. Now, I'm from the inner city, so I know how inner-city kids look. They often have little holes in their shirts and jeans. Maybe their shoes are worn out a little bit. So, there we were, right across from this table filled with sweet little kids and the two moms.

Why did they happen to be right in front of me? No idea, but I couldn't help but notice that the mom who had her back to me was running her finger down the right side of the menu, as I always did for my whole life: how much did it cost, and what do you get for it? And there I was, looking at the left side of the menu for the first time.

To this day, I don't know why I did it, but after some quick calculations (twelve kids plus two adults) and I thought what was the worst damage they could do? Ten to fifteen dollars apiece? Hey, I had two-thousand dollars. I followed the waiter into the kitchen and said, "Go back out there and tell those ladies at that table to order whatever they want. Someone's going to pick up the bill plus your fifteen percent tip, but don't tell them who," and then I went back and sat down.

For me with no money, a ten percent tip would have been a big deal. Fifteen percent? Wow, that was big time!

The waiter went over and spoke to one of the women. She stood up, such a grand lady, and slowly began looking around the room. When her gaze came to me, her expression said, "No, it can't be that guy," and she continued to look around. It was a big restaurant. Who could it be? With her back to me, she raised her hands and, in a very loud, angelic voice said, "Whoever you are . . ." and everyone in the restaurant stopped and looked at her. "Whoever you are, God bless you. You have no idea what you're doing for me and these children. No idea, but God bless you." As she said those words, chills went up and down my body. Goose bumps. And suddenly I felt as high as a kite. Now I was around in the sixties, when all of us were trying to get high as a kite, but that was nothing compared to this. And I stayed that way for a couple days!

Doing something for somebody and asking nothing in return gives me or any of us the biggest reward imaginable: the satisfaction that comes from knowing you've made the world a better place because you were here. And those women and children never knew who paid for that dinner.

When you do something for someone else and don't expect anything in return . . . you get the greatest high!

Our Little Company Starts to Grow

In our third year, we did 3.4 million dollars in business, still running the office from my house, with Shirley Wong picking up the phone and saying, "John Paul Mitchell Systems hair care products, how can I help you?"

It was about five years before we had a real office and got our own warehouse. By then, we were selling over thirty million a year and had about twenty employees.

Over the next five years, we developed several additional products and started to advertise a little, mainly to the trade publications. It was the late 1980s before we expanded our advertising to the general public.

Looking back, we realized that losing our investor was a blessing in disguise. It meant that Paul and I were the sole owners of JPMS, answering only to ourselves and maintaining our vision for the company. Even though we started our business during an economic recession, we barely noticed. We had no time to watch TV or listen to the news. We never lived beyond our means, and we carefully managed every expense. We were always doing something, just trying to survive. We believed in our product and focused on managing our money well.

Sometimes success comes down to where you choose to focus. If you give twenty percent of your time to this, thirty percent of your time to that, and the rest to something else, you are tri-focused. We gave one-hundred percent to our business. Even during the worst of times, there is always opportunity.

Little Did We Know

In the early days, Paul and I thought that if we were ever lucky enough to do five million a year in business, we could make a couple hundred thousand dollars each and be the happiest guys in the world. Little did we know that it would go up much, much more.

The year we did 3.4 million dollars in business, we had no doubt that we could easily do ten or fifteen million. As we started approaching that, we knew we could easily reach the next level: one-hundred million dollars! And then one day we realized we could possibly have a billion-dollar business.

What really made it happen was two things. We loved the professional beauty industry and we loved giving the public products we were proud of.

Our products were great and people loved them. All of a sudden, our business took off and we became the fastest-growing company in the United States in the professional beauty industry. It was unreal.

I encourage you to celebrate every little win in your business. Not just with yourself, but with others in your community. Sure, we worked hard to get there, but lots of people helped us along the way. That's why I titled this book, *Success Unshared is Failure*.

Chapter 6

A Formula for Success

You can't go into business without having a plan or formula for success. From the start, Paul Mitchell and I wanted to offer luxury hair care at an affordable price. We also wanted input from hairdressers when it came to adding and improving our products. The bottom line: we wanted to be the best and most popular professional hair care brand for stylists. We always wanted to be there for them and their salons, no matter what they needed.

Being open to change over time is also important for a successful business, whether it's upgrading our management style or introducing new products. We've done both. We've also learned our lesson about dealing with rejection. God knows we've had our share. But we just keep ignoring it and plowing ahead. I think it's worked pretty well for us so far.

Of course, giving to those less fortunate has always been a part of our plan too. We involve our salons and schools as much as possible and many of them have their own fundraising projects.

Upgrading Our Management

After a few years, we knew we needed to hire someone to manage our business. It was 1989 and our company was about nine years old. We were growing crazy fast, and it was getting harder to keep up with our business operations. Paul was very ill, and I was trying to take on more and more. We brought in an outside consulting firm to tell us what we needed to do to stay on track. They gave us a report, but we needed someone who had a management background to read and evaluate the report. My friend John Capra suggested somebody he knew, a guy by the name of Luke Jacobellis.

Luke read the report, and we discussed it. Lucky for us, he was leaving his job, so I offered him a position as our distribution manager and he accepted. He started in May of 1989. It was the same month that Paul passed away. Luke has been with the company ever since, until he retired a couple of years ago. But he stayed around long enough to help train our new leaders.

Luke Jacobellis and Me

Photo courtesy of author's personal collection

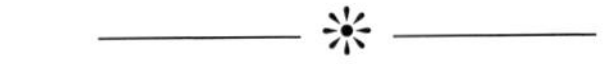

From Luke Jacobellis

In 1989, I was working in management at Xerox. I'd been there for sixteen years and was ready to make a move. John Capra, a good friend of mine, told me that his friend needed advice about managing his business. Although I knew about the nice gifts John Paul DeJoria would give to John every Christmas, I'd never met him or Paul Mitchell. I didn't even know there was such a thing as a professional hair industry. I met JP at his home to review his report from an outside consulting firm. After a while he said, "I understand you're leaving your job." I said "Yeah." Then he offered me a management position at JPMS. He asked how much I was making at Xerox. I told him and he said, "Fine. We'll start with that and we'll go up from there." And he kept his word multiple times during the next thirty-five years.

You have to understand; John Paul is one of those unique people. He's very good with numbers, but his wheelhouse is sales and marketing. Paul Mitchell was the guy whose name was on the bottle. With Paul sick and dying, John Paul now had the burden of figuring out how to carry the company forward. That's why he needed me. Any number of guys could have done what I did. I was just blessed to be in the right place at the right time.

I started as the distribution manager, then became the operations guy, followed by general manager, and finally I was on the board of directors, all within the first year. As JP got comfortable with me and I got to understand him better, I learned how to run his business, according to John Paul DeJoria. What's his vision? I would ask. What's his culture? Then I incorporated them into the operational pieces that I had to put together.

No business is more important to JP than JPMS, but he has his fingers in a lot of other pies. Over time, he got more comfortable with me and would give up a little bit more. First, he gave up the education side of it, then the marketing side, then the sales side. By the late-90s, I was running the whole thing as CEO and President. Then my job became to groom our younger people in the right direction so they could take over. I was good for the business, and the business was very good to me. It was a win-win all the way. And we had a great ride.

Quality and Affordable Products

From the start we knew product quality was important to us, and it would be a big part of our success. We never made products for the consumer. We made them for our hairdressers to approve, because hairdressers know what hair needs. The consumer wants to know, how does it smell? How's it been advertised? Will it feel okay on my hair? Because we make our products for hairdressers, we make sure the quality is so good the hairdresser will want to use it over and over again, and, of course, recommend it to their customers. Even if the industry changes, we always want to benefit salons, one way or another.

A great example of this are our first three products: Shampoo One, Shampoo Two, and The Conditioner. We still sell them over forty years later. Normally you go through products every three years and you change them out. So, our products had to have staying power. The quality had to be there for us to be in the reorder business. Reorders were really important to us because we had no money back then.

Overcoming Rejection and Being a Good Listener

I think one of the biggest philosophies that has driven our success over the years—from the very beginning—is that I learned how to overcome rejection. That's something you're going to get, and in many cases, you need to learn to ignore it. We got so much negative input in the early years. People saying, "This isn't going to happen." But life is like that. Some of the lessons I learned when I sold encyclopedias door to door still hold true today. You're going to get a lot of rejection. If you know it's coming, it's easier to ignore. All you need to do is keep your mind on your goal. This is very helpful when people are telling you you're not going to make it.

But the more important lesson is learning how to listen and give people what they want. That means looking at problems from their perspective as opposed to your point of view. Old style business was, "I'm the boss. You do it because I say so." Management these days is about looking at how we can make it better. Asking how we can help. We go straight to our salons, especially with a new product, and say "Hey, we're thinking of coming out with this. What do you think?" We go to our staff and ask them too. Sometimes they come to us and make suggestions about new products. They feel free to make changes to what management suggests, then explain why. Usually, we agree with them once we take a good look at their side. We don't make decisions for ego's sake but for a good end result. We incorporate other people in what we do so the outcome is a team effort.

Being a listener is very important. There are lots of times I think I'm right and my staff turns my mind totally around.

You need to listen to what others tell you and be open to incorporating their ideas and advice.

Supporting Our Hairdressers

Everything we do supports the hairdressers. Not just making the products, but how we help them display it. We knew from experience how most companies in this industry come into these shops and promise they'll stay supporting hairdressers forever. Pretty soon they become big retail product producers and they've forgotten who got them there. Our promise, and we meant it, was we'd stay behind the hairdresser indefinitely in any way we could and include them in all we do. That's our job. What we knew from the start was that we wanted to, and hopefully could, support the industry no matter how distribution changes.

Including Our Salons and Schools in Philanthropy

Because of my success with John Paul Mitchell Systems, I was able to invest in real estate and start companies like Patrón. Those investments have made it possible for me to follow my philosophy of "success unshared is failure" in a big way all over the world. I explain in detail what we've accomplished later in the book, but I'll give you a small taste of it now.

I've financed programs such as feeding the hungry, finding new water sources for farmers, saving the ocean reefs and sea life, supporting orphans, veterans, and the homeless, and working toward a better and healthier world, just to name a few. I'm especially proud of the fact that from the beginning,

John Paul Mitchell Systems was one of the first cosmetology companies to publicly stand up against animal testing.

One thing we started early with the company, and continue to this day, is including our Paul Mitchell School students and hairdressers at our sports marketing and philanthropy events throughout the United States and now the world. We always invite them to come because these sponsorships are usually attached to a charity. Our students volunteer their time doing people's hair. It's a great way for them to share what they learned at the Paul Mitchell School. Their getting involved helps people look better, feel better, and it also helps raise money and attention for a cause.

When I do a lot of my promotional events or a lot of my philanthropy, I say "On behalf of hairdressers, we are doing this." For example, we have partnered with Food 4 Africa in South Africa to provide food to communities and kids in schools. Our Paul Mitchell students jump in holding fundraisers for these causes, and it makes a huge difference. The salons do too. People see that and want to be associated with it.

We include our salons in a lot of our activities. I was in New York City for the launch of The John Paul DeJoria. This is a ship for the Captain Paul Watson Foundation. He was a co-founder of Greenpeace and has spent fifty years being an important conservation advocate and researcher all over the world. He left the Sea Shepherd Foundation and started the Captain Paul Watson Foundation. I bought him this ship (later I bought him another ship and he called it Bandero) so he could continue the good work he does, defending whales, dolphins, sharks, turtles, and other sea life. Not only did the ship come in—right in front of the Statue of Liberty—but I invited hairdressers and my local distributor from New York and New Jersey to participate. When we do fun things, we invite our customers and support team to come and be part of these events too.

Almost everything we do, we do on behalf of our salon owners and stylists, and we tell them what we've done. Then they tell their customers. It's a source of pride for them to be able to say "We're part of John Paul Mitchell Systems and look at what we're doing in Africa. Look at what we're doing to save the whales. Look at what we're doing in Appalachia. Look at what we're doing for the homeless in Austin and Los Angeles." So, we share it with them, and they share it with their customers. They're part of bigger purpose. Part of a huge, beautiful, positive movement.

Early Milestone

To this day, my most memorable milestone was paying all our bills on time after two years in business. But there are others that bring a smile to my face. I clearly remember our first million-dollar month. I was in Europe on a little vacation. I called my general manager and asked him, "How's everything going down there?" He said, "JP, we had our first million-dollar month." My reaction was "Oh, my God. This is unbelievable. And I'm out of town." I just jumped up and down for days. That was a big milestone.

No one thought a company like ours could ever make it to fifty million dollars, let alone one-hundred million dollars. So, another milestone was the year we made our first one-hundred million dollars. From that time on, we started looking bigger. We even talked about one day becoming a billion-dollar-company. Eventually, we did that too.

95

Chapter 7

Losing a Partner and a Friend

Paul Mitchell and Me
Photo courtesy of author's personal collection

The minute Paul Mitchell and I met in 1972, we became best friends and hung out together. He was a real gentleman. When he came back to the mainland from Hawaii in the 1970s, he would always stay in my home. A lot of his old friends were happy to see him back. We made a great team during the early years of John Paul Mitchell Systems. He had amazing chemistry on stage, and I loved selling our products. But no matter how much business we did, we always had fun. That's because we did what we loved and we loved what we did.

Paul was a big draw when it came to hair shows, but he was surprisingly modest about his ability to cut hair. I remember what he told me at the International Beauty Show we did in Atlanta, Georgia. Paul was on a big stage on the main floor. There were probably about a thousand people watching and listening to him. I said to Paul afterwards, "You must be the greatest haircutter the world's ever known."

Paul said, "JP, I want to show you something." We walked into a ballroom where his friend Maurice Tidy was cutting hair. I was amazed. The room was big enough for 250 people but only twelve people were there. They were all sitting in the front row watching every move Maurice Tidy made. He played music but didn't talk. He just did hair. Paul said, "That guy is probably the best stylist I've seen in my whole life. You want to know the difference between him and me? I can talk and he can't. I talk to my people on stage and afterwards. I hang out with them. But only the great ones know how great Maurice is."

And here's another great memory. Paul and I built a solar-energy wind car (the Mana La) on our Awapuhi farm in Hawaii. We entered the world's first solar car race across Australia. We had so much fun trading off as drivers and we did well. The Mana La is displayed at the famous Petersen Automotive Museum in Los Angeles.

A Final Word from Paul

About a month before Paul died, he and I had some time together. He'd been doing a show with three other artists on stage and we were back at the hotel across the street. "JP, it's not looking good," he said. "But I want to tell you what makes me feel good. Across the street are three hairdressers and I trained them all." One was Jeanne Braa and the other was a young man named Robert Cromeans. The third was a guy named Albie Mulcahy. "JP, I trained all three of them," he repeated, "and they're as good as I am. As a trainer, I've created three of the greatest hair stylists." He looked at me with a big smile on his face. "Are you going to move forward doing all of our shows together with them?" What a moment.

From Robert Cromeans

I was twenty-four years old when I saw JP and Paul Mitchell for the first time. It was on a VHS tape when I was in beauty school so I guess you could call it a digital experience. I fell in love with Paul Mitchell. He was Scottish. I was Scottish. He thought he was funny. I thought I was funny. From that day on, I sort of believed in something for the first time. We're talking about thirty-eight years ago. There was this cool guy with a ponytail driving his Porsche through somewhere in California which was beyond any dream I had. That was JP. But Paul was something else. He was a controversial hairdresser who would do unusual things. He was also very much a showman. A lot of what I've done over my last thirty-eight years was inspired by him. And I did get to work with him on his very last show before he passed.

Prepared for the Worst

Paul's death in 1989 was a critical time for me and JPMS. Paul was my friend. When he passed, when he left his human body, I lost a friend and a darn good business partner. It affected me as it would anyone. Even though I understood he had left his body and was going on to bigger and better things, I felt that loss. He was a great guy and I was lucky to have him in my life. Like Paul, I also wanted the business we'd started together to continue growing.

Paul had pancreatic cancer and several other problems. From a business standpoint we were prepared for the worst, because we had almost a year knowing things weren't so good for him. That made it easier. Up until then, Paul Mitchell was the face of our company. I had to work harder that year and the next couple of years to get my face in front of everybody. It was important that our clients and providers still felt the personal touch that Paul had delivered, and it was my job to make that happen. I used to explain, "I'm the John Paul in John Paul Mitchell Systems. How do you do," and let it go at that. Once we discovered how serious his health concerns were, I started doing more presentations, spent more time in front of the people we were working with, and began to put myself in ads.

Luke Jacobellis

When JP lost Paul he knew our bread and butter was in the salon industry, not in selling bottles of shampoo to the consumer. As long as we were committed to the salon business, the rest would fall into place. And that's exactly what happened. He brought in people—maybe not yet of Paul's status—but well-respected people in the hair industry. People like Jeanne Braa, Paul's girlfriend who'd been working with him, John and Suzanne Chadwick, Scott Cole, Linda Yodice, Robert Cromeans (another Scottish-born hairdresser). They helped JP continue Paul's legacy. Many of them became icons in their own right.

When Paul died, the industry assumed that losing the hairdresser partner would cause JPMS to fall apart. Much to their surprise, it didn't happen. I immediately went out and started talking to the public, hairdressers, and other groups, and we continued to grow. Not only did we survive, but we thrived. The industry realized that we were here to stay. The same principles we had when Paul and I started the company were still there—and so was I.

Angus Mitchell

Paul's son, Angus, was still pretty young when his father died, but his exposure to the hair industry inspired the same passion his father had for it. He was educated at Vidal Sassoon and created his own signature style, eventually taking over for his father at JPMS. Since Paul was one of my best friends, I knew Angus most of his life. He was a great partner to work with. He was also a well-trained and skilled hairdresser who became a well-known platform artist and educator, doing several major shows a year to educate hairdressers. And he was a model and spokesperson for our men's line MITCH. On top of that, Angus did public relations work for JPMS, including talking at many of the schools, and he was, of course, on the board of directors.

Inspired by the loss of his father, Angus did philanthropic work with PanCAN, a foundation dedicated to advancing research, supporting patients and creating hope for anyone affected by pancreatic cancer. He also was an advocate for environmental research and preservation. In 2007, he donated a historic coastal property in Hawaii valued at 6.5 million dollars to the Nature Conservancy, in hopes that Hawaiians would see it as a place of serenity where they could also walk in history.

Unfortunately, Angus passed away a few months after I began this book. The amazing thing is that he was exactly the same age as Paul was when he died—fifty-three years old. Angus Mitchell was an honest man with a heart full of love. I could never have asked for a better friend and partner.

From Robert Cromeans

In the past five or six years, I got very close to Angus, partly because he and I shared a love for his father. Also, I think I was holding his place for him until he was ready. And then we actually became partners in doing the shows, just like I'd been with Jeanne Braa after Paul died. I would never go to a show without Angus. When he was doing hair, he was very focused, and I loved that. I had the owner of this incredible company on stage, cutting hair. Angus worked and communicated with his heart. You just knew he'd probably hugged every hairdresser in the industry. He was that way. Angus and I became best buddies. And it's not just the connection with Paul. We loved doing shows. We loved inspiring hairdressers. We didn't mind traveling. And we did it with grace and style. It's our culture, the culture of JPMS. It's who we are.

Chapter 8
Taking Care of My People

There were many times when I worked for other people where maybe I had a dollar for lunch, right? You can't get a lot for a dollar, not even twenty, thirty, forty, or fifty years ago. I decided that as soon as we made enough money—and it took a few years to do this—anyone that worked in our office or warehouse was going to get free lunch. I think we put that in effect, maybe our fifth year in business. It was something we could afford then and now. So, it's still in practice today.

You work at Paul Mitchell, and you get a subsidized lunch every day. Everyone who works in our office and our warehouse gets to order off a menu and choose what they want. That was one thing I instigated and never changed. I've always kept that going.

And when people needed various working hours because of situations in their families or their lives, we would work with them to find a flexible way to accommodate their needs. Maybe work from home a day or two and the rest of the time come into the office. We started that thirty years ago to give people a helping hand with their own lives.

We also made sure that if they did a good job, they not only had a nice salary, but also yearly bonuses and profit-sharing money. As we grew, it could go into a retirement fund for them, and they could have quite a bit of money by retirement age. From the profit sharing we did with them, their 401(k)s, and social security as well, they could have a decent life after they retired. And that has worked well for everyone.

We also have an open policy at JPMS. Staff can talk to me anytime they want. If you ever have a problem you get stuck with, pick up the phone and call me. It works pretty well. I don't get many phone calls.

---- ※ ----

From Luke Jacobellis

I have fond memories of JP going out to the warehouse and hanging out with the guys, even helping them drive the pallet jack around. He wants to spend his moment saying hi to everybody. What can I do for you? Is everything okay? And I love you guys and thanks for doing what you do for me.

---- ※ ----

Five Super-pals: CB Sullivan, John Capra, Gary Spellman, Me, and Luke Jacobellis at a JPMS distributor meeting in Hawaii

Photo courtesy of author's personal collection

Building a Team

When we started John Paul Mitchell Systems, we had no employees, obviously, because it was just Paul and I. As the company grew, we were able to start hiring—first one person, then more people over time. Occasionally we would bring in outside consultants, but almost all of our senior positions were filled by promotions from within the company. It is nice to promote from within, and it is still something we do proudly and regularly. We love both fostering the growth of our team members as well as hiring from outside the company because we like giving opportunity to everybody! Your existing team knows the culture, the relationships, and is personally invested in the company's success because they helped build it. Alternately, someone from the outside comes in with a fresh perspective, information, and experience that is new to us, and a different kind of excitement for growth and change. It is the combination of both that is important, because it means we are always learning from one another, while never losing the footing of who we are at the soul of our business. We have the finest team there is, not only because they are the best and brightest, but they are all very good people who care about the success of the company and one another. And *that* is what truly builds the strongest team.

Creating a Sales Force

One of the challenges of growing was building a sales force. When we started, Paul and I were it. That wasn't going to work once we got bigger. To build up a salesforce, I went to as many of our large seminars as I possibly could to get people excited about JPMS so we could train them as presenters.

Every year, we would do a major seminar in Las Vegas for three thousand of the top stylists and salons. Then we'd do another one for 2,000 of our students. When there were major shows in different parts of the United States, I'd try to attend and speak about the industry. I'd share how we at John Paul Mitchell Systems were helping to change how business was done through our schools and charitable activities. I still do major events today.

Each year I fly all over the world to many of our regional meetings. Regional for me used to mean areas of the United States. Now we bring people together in Asia, Europe, North and South America, Africa, and other places. I attend most of those major events. It's amazing to reflect on how we've grown.

Going International

There were a lot of things I had to learn when we jumped into the international market. I had to learn about international financing. I had to learn about converting currency from other countries into ours. I had to calculate what the shipping fees would be and had to determine duty charges. Many countries do things really differently than others. It was an education.

I was blessed having a fellow named Leslie Spears out of England, one of my first international distributors. He spent time with me explaining how everything is done a bit differently in the international market. I listened. And I learned. It took a long time and I'm still learning today, but we're expanding more and more now in the international market because of that early education Leslie gave to me.

Pandemic Challenges

We've never forgotten how important hairdressers are to our business–back then and today. That's why we've always done things to show our salons how much we appreciate their support.

COVID created a huge problem for us. As you can imagine, salons were particularly hard-hit by the pandemic. Everyone was going after all these loans from the government. We didn't. We heard that many salons went for that extra money but were waiting in line and didn't get it. So, we wrote a letter to the government saying that we qualified, but we weren't going to ask for any money whatsoever. Instead, we said, please move salons to the front of your list.

When salons started coming back again, they had little to no money. They'd been shut down in some cases for months at a time. My then partner, Angus Mitchell, and I made a decision to help salons out. We took millions of our own dollars, bought product for the backbar and color, and gave it to them free of charge—to put them back in business again. We also gave our distributors extended dating with the salons. When they reordered, they didn't have to pay right away.

Because of the supply shortage we experienced after the pandemic, there was a month we were back-ordered tens of millions of dollars. We had the orders but didn't have the product. We made a big decision then, not to take any profits out of the company. We left it all in to build up our inventories for our hairdressing salons. For more than two years Angus and I took zero dividends out of the company. We built gigantic inventories to help our customers out. We'll get back to profit eventually, but it's people before profit when the industry needs help to grow. We don't want our salons losing money or our customers if there's something we can do to prevent that.

Chapter 9
Our Products

When we started in 1980, all we had were two shampoos and a conditioner. I mentioned earlier that Ron DiSalvo improved Paul's original formulas for our shampoos and conditioner. Ron and I had been good buddies at Redken, and he was doing consulting work at the time. Because of our friendship, he generously recreated our new formulas for free. Our original shampoos and conditioner are still sold today, which says a lot about the quality of our products.

Sculpting Lotion

A few months into our business, Paul found a setting lotion that he really liked. "It doesn't flake," he said. "You can put it on hair and it doesn't flake. Boy if we had this, we could do some great things." It was the start of our Sculpting Lotion and the "wet look" which Paul became famous for. It's a small product now, but it was revolutionary in the early 80s. It was a hairdressing tool that hardened, allowing the hairdresser to work the hair and create a style.

If you comb your hair back or put waves in, it looks like it's wet, but it's really dry. It's the same if you have curly hair and just scrunch it up. I thought great, but we needed to create our own formula. So, I bought it. And I figured out with another cosmetic chemist how to recreate it, except for one ingredient, Quaternium-23. I called the company personally, introduced myself, and asked how much of the ingredient was in their lotion. They told me it was less than five percent. So, I had the chemist try different amounts of the ingredient in his lab until we found the perfect amount. In the 90s we came up with an even better version called Super Sculpt.

Of course, Paul had to use the Sculpting Lotion while we were trying out the right proportion of ingredients. It was still a few months into the business, and we'd booked a show at the Biltmore Hotel in LA. Paul was using the sculpting lotion. Now remember, we're still experimenting with it. He was on stage, putting pin curls in the model's hair with his fingers while talking to people. This particular formula dried so fast that one half was dry before the other half was started. The formula was still too strong. It was pretty funny because he'd planned to wave brush it out. Paul started to laugh. "By the way, I put our new experimental sculpting lotion on this side to see how hard it would get. Oh my God, look how hard it gets." Then he showed them the difference between the two sides. Paul was great at making a mistake look as if it were deliberate.

In over forty-five years since we started John Paul Mitchell Systems, we've added many products. And you can buy them in over one hundred countries around the world. All our products today are made with the highest-quality ingredients and the newest technologies. We have licensed hairdressers working together with first-rate formulators to make every new product perfect. Being eco-friendly is important to us. Whenever possible, we look for natural and sustainable ingredients to put in our products and use the latest environmentally sensitive practices in packaging.

Chapter 10

Our Salons and Our Shows

When we started John Paul Mitchell Systems in 1980, I went around to salons, explaining the benefits of our products. But we did more than that. I would travel the country, contacting potential distributors and convincing them to put on shows and seminars for salon owners and their hairdressers. Paul and Jeanne would follow me and perform at these shows, doing the latest haircuts and styles with our products. We would teach hairdressers how to present and sell our products by using them on their clients and sending them home with the ability to recreate what they'd done in the salons. Having someone buy the product once wasn't enough. We didn't have a lot of money, so we needed to create a reorder business.

The Early Shows

Getting salon owners and hairdressers to our shows was crucial for our business. But since we were broke, some of the early shows we did had to be pretty creative. I remember the first one we did in LA. We found out when the Biltmore Hotel in downtown LA had a day they weren't using their main auditorium, and we asked them to host a hair show for us. We told them we'd pay right after. Robert Clegg, a friend of ours, had published a book with Paul about his haircuts and some of the other things he did. He let us have a hundred copies upfront. "Let me help you out here," he said. "Just pay me later. I know you're good for it." So, we told everybody around that Paul Mitchell was going to have a big show. Paul was well known back then from the other shows he'd done with me, and we ended up with a couple hundred people there, which was quite amazing. Friends of ours pitched in with flowers and a tablecloth, and someone brought a few little hors d'oeuvres. Paul and I did the show with Jeanne Braa, and I sold enough books to be able to pay for the room. And that's how we got our first big start there in LA.

From the beginning, we had Paul do shows all around the United States. I remember one we did in Pennsylvania. Because it was the early days, we had no lights. We had nothing! Our distributor had found a little location for us where maybe fewer than a hundred hairdressers showed up. We had a stage but no lighting. We even had to borrow a chair from the salon. Paul and I went through the back of this old hotel and found a couple of old lights made out of aluminum that were all banged up and had been thrown away. We straightened them out a bit, bought 120-watt bulbs to put in them, added little clamps, and attached them to a pole we found. They became the lights for the stage. I'll never forget it. But we still put on a great show. We let everybody know we were starting out and, just like them, wanted to make our American dream come true. We promised one day we'd have better lights. And of course, one day we had great lights. That was a fun show. We laughed our heads off.

Paul was popular from doing shows before John Paul Mitchell Systems, so we got booked. However, Paul and I were the only ones getting paid to do a show. Here's how we worked around it. Let's say we got paid $1,000 to do a show, but they also gave us round-trip air tickets and a hotel suite to stay in. This was perfect for us. We'd cash in our tickets and buy two of the cheapest tickets together at midnight. We had a room to stay in and were really good buddies. We'd switch up. One night, he would have the bedroom, and I would get the couch in the living room. The next night, we'd switch over again. Paul and I went into business by using whatever we had, and we'd laugh about it. We laughed a lot together.

Most of the shows, we'd make just enough to put them on and pay the people who helped us. There was really no money left over for us. But we could sell our products at the shows and that's how we got our product line going. We showed hairdressers how to use them and how to show their customers the way to use them. And it worked out quite nicely. The moneymaker was never the show. The moneymaker was selling the product and picking up two more salons. Whatever we made at the shows went to our distributors to pay their expenses.

Staff and artists of John Paul Mitchell Systems at our 2018 gathering event in Las Vegas

Photo courtesy of JPMS

While Paul was alive, our personal shows weren't too big. We'd do shows for about a thousand people here and there. But after he died, I thought it was important to get as many people together as possible. These were first class shows for three thousand people, often in Las Vegas. People would pay a couple hundred bucks to attend and pay for their own hotel rooms, but their meals and other stuff were included. We'd bring the Las Vegas glamour to our shows. It would cost us probably about a couple of million dollars a year. Then we did the same thing with our Paul Mitchell School students.

From Luke Jacobellis

When Paul was dying, JP became the face of the company. After a while, we started to have big educational events for the salon industry. We called them Gatherings and ours were the biggest. We'd bring in stylists and hairdressers and salon owners to these events by the thousands, and JP would lead because he's a very dynamic speaker. He didn't pretend to be the hairdresser. No. He was the leader who was devoted to the hair industry.

It would cost us millions to put these things on. They were the cost of doing business. They'd show our commitment to the salons and keep them connected to us and believing in us. They were primarily about education and training. After JP, others would speak including some of our own people. Then attendees would go into breakout rooms where they'd learn the latest techniques in color, styling, perms, and retailing to the consumer.

At the same time, JP started to advertise in magazines and on tv commercials. He began to make a name for himself. And his energy level was unbelievable. It still is today. Although he started to branch into other industries, the salon industry is always number one for him. It's the salon industry that made him and he's never going to turn his back on them.

It started out with me as the figurehead and with Jeanne Braa and Robert Cromeans as the top stylists. It wasn't long before Jeanne Braa—and especially Robert Cromeans—became superstars, and other top educators worked with us along the way. Our shows became even bigger and better.

We just expanded from doing those shows. I did more and more advertising and jumped into the world of television. We started using models too. It was around that time in 1991 that my wife Eloise and I got together, and she started modeling for JPMS. She did such a great job that she became our corporate spokesmodel in 1992. Most every ad we did for the next twenty-five years featured Eloise. Women would bring Eloise's picture from some of those ads to their hairdresser and say, "Make me look like this!"

It was around this time that JPMS really exploded. After I became the new face of the company, people would stop me thinking I was Paul Mitchell. They'd ask, "How are you doing, Paul?"

I would respond, "No, no, I'm the John Paul in John Paul Mitchell Systems. Paul was my partner, a great hairdresser. Just call me JP for John Paul."

From Robert Cromeans

Whenever I did a show during the 1980s, I'd run up to JP and say, "Hey, John Paul. I'm Robert Cromeans." I think he found me weird at first. Then at one event, I popped my chair by him the way I usually did, and he said, "Oh, I know who you are. You'd be the next Paul Mitchell." It was as if he'd given me a target to go for after I'd lost my mentor. I was really too young to be the next hairdresser on deck, but my name came up at a board meeting. The opinion was that I was too young, and then somebody said, "How many classes has he done?" The answer was that I'd done forty classes in the last month. John Paul said, "That sounds like the artistic director I want." And our relationship was built from that.

My job was to build hair shows. As time went on, the shows got bigger and bigger. They didn't just involve a couple dozen models. We also created lots of music and clever videos. They were like mini rock concerts. At our big shows in Vegas, my job was to reveal JP. Once, I did it with motorcycles. I also had him fly through the air. There's nothing he won't do because he doesn't take himself too seriously.

Now we service over a hundred thousand salons worldwide. In the United States, we probably service about forty to fifty thousand. But the salons that are really into the Paul Mitchell culture number about six or seven thousand. By culture I don't mean how the salons sell our products. I mean how they give back. At our Gatherings, we have classes for our hairdressers and salon owners on how to work better with people and how to be a better hairdresser. We also include our salons in our philanthropy, although they often have their own philanthropy which is great. We urge people to give back and include them in events we do, whether it's skiing or going to the ocean. We have surfers take children who are autistic or have MS out on surfboards and it changes their life. Some of our people from Germany and the United States went to Africa to volunteer for Food 4 Africa. It encourages people to see more of the world and to understand the challenges that others have. It just makes them better people.

**JP's entrance at one of the JPMS Gathering events;
Every year he did something different**

Photo courtesy of JPMS

From Robert Cromeans

Since I have my own salon, one of my jobs at the shows was to teach salon owners how to run their businesses. I taught people that hairdressing isn't just about the hair. We don't cut with dolls, we cut with people. I showed them how to get clients and keep them for life. I asked them if they were out there trying to attract people. I showed them how to build their teams and ways to build clients' salon experiences. I taught them to have a consultation every step of the way. If you handle the experience well, it will bring you bigger tips, return business, word-of-mouth business, treatment sales, and what I like to call take-home sales.

I used to have seven salons, but as I grew older and my leases ran out, I couldn't keep up with them. I still have my flagship salon in San Diego and it's glorious. Our color bar is under a glass dome, and we do our shampoos in the dark. We try to make it a spa-like experience. We have vibrating chairs and do a lot with face masks and hot towels. Once you've gone through your shampoo experience, you know the rest will be good. I like to think I've inspired people to Walk the Walk. When I go spying on Paul Mitchell salons in South Africa or salons in Kentucky, they look exactly like mine. I recently visited a salon in Aswan that I inspired twenty years ago. They've got blow dryers that hang from the ceiling and slide down as if they're from heaven. They had a color bar, a lather lounge, and a wash house. This salon is one of the top businesses in the country.

While COVID prices have gone up around the country, salons have been reluctant to increase their prices. Here's a solution. When you increase your price, then just increase the experience. Don't give your client the same experience she had last time. Give her a new one. They say you can lead a horse to water, but you can't make it drink. My job is to add salt to their diet! It's as simple as that.

Chapter 11
The Paul Mitchell Schools

Education was also a big part of the vision Paul and I had. That's why I started the Paul Mitchell Schools. Not right away, of course. We needed to build our business first. But we were always thinking about our future and the future of the beauty industry. Like everything else in the world, the beauty industry was always changing, and we wanted to be a part of those changes. The hair industry is very different now from the way it was when we started out. Part of our dream was to educate new generations of hairdressers in all the latest methods of hairstyling, makeup, and color.

Sometimes good ideas and the people who know how to bring them to life just fall in your lap. That's what happened when we hired Winn Claybaugh as a motivational speaker at our shows back in 1989. He had a few salons and his own school at the time, so he knew about the importance of education for hairdressers. Winn was a popular speaker, and other companies hired him too. One day I told him, "If you don't want to be exclusive to us, that's okay. But I will book you so much that you won't have time to work for any other company." After that Winn became more and more visible under the JPMS banner.

I said that Winn Claybaugh fell into our lap, but it was another ten years before we took full advantage of his talents. I'd been trying to come up with different systems and curriculums that would support existing beauty schools, but they weren't working. Then I had someone check out Winn's Beauty School in Provo, Utah, and she was impressed. I finally decided to talk to an expert and approached Winn about opening up beauty schools for JPMS. He said that he'd love to help, so I offered him a great partnership which I knew he was looking for. "Okay. I'm fifty percent and you're fifty percent. We'll be equal partners." In 2001, we opened our first Paul Mitchell School in Costa Mesa, California. Our original plan was to open about seven schools around the country. Here we are almost twenty-five years later, and we have schools in over 100 locations all over the country. And my partner, Winn Claybaugh, is the dean of all our schools.

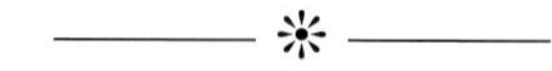

From Winn Claybaugh

Forty years ago, I opened my first school, the Von Curtis Academy in Provo, Utah, and fell in love with the school business. I opened up several salons earlier, so I was already in love with the beauty business. But it was the education side of it I loved the most. As if I didn't have enough to do, I also became a successful motivational speaker, which is how I ended up working with JPMS. I felt as if I had the credibility to talk about beauty education because I practiced and implemented the same ideas within my own company. When JP asked me to help him open up Paul Mitchell Schools, I was thrilled. I can't believe I had the nerve to tell him I wanted to be a partner. But JP is a very generous man, and he agreed on the spot.

Between the two of us, we basically changed the model of

beauty schools. Most schools back then were mom and pop type operations. They taught whatever was necessary for students to pass the state board exam, which was often outdated with the skill set students were required to learn. Many hairdressers didn't even learn how to cut hair until they started working in salons. And yet the career opportunities that existed in the professional beauty industry, and still do, are overwhelming. Most salons are understaffed. So, the idea of opening schools that offer serious training was welcome.

I couldn't have made a better decision to ask for Winn's help. He believed in our business philosophy of caring and giving back, and he shaped the culture of the Paul Mitchell Schools to follow those goals. By sharing our business philosophy, he also inspires audiences of beauty professionals across America to become more successful.

The Paul Mitchell Schools are franchises that are independently owned and operated, although we own a percentage of some. We've never had to recruit partners for our schools. There's usually some kind of relationship with JPMS. Some of them were distributors of JPMS products before they became school owners. One partner was the top Paul Mitchell salon owner in her state. She heard about the school opportunity and now owns several. Think about it. What better way to support your salons than to train hairdressers yourself? They're all part of the Paul Mitchell School network and offer the best educational foundation needed to start a career in the beauty industry.

From Winn Claybaugh

From the start, we knew that having a system was important for running a school. People don't run our schools. There's too much room for error. But people do work the systems that run our schools. The foundation for our system evolved from the way JP used to run JPMS and the fifteen years of experience I had in running an award-winning cosmetology school. We had a curriculum that we knew from experience, worked. We also believe in flexibility which means our system and our curriculum is a living, breathing structure that we constantly tweak and refine.

We had a great name brand—Paul Mitchell—and we had a great cutting curriculum. What made us different though was our culture. We based our culture on what I call these three basic human needs. The first is that people need to feel safe. The second is that people need to feel that they belong. The third basic human need is that people need to have a purpose. Let me explain that third one. One school janitor cleans because it's his job and someone pays him to do it. The other school janitor cleans because it's his privilege to create a clean learning environment for the next generation that's going to save the planet. The first janitor has a job, but the second janitor has a purpose. There's nobody better than JP at creating that culture. That's why our students are so loyal, and nobody ever wants to leave JPMS. And we are very specific about what we do to create those three things.

With all of that in mind, we decided to make our schools look like beautiful salons. We had our students dress like professional hairdressers. After a while, we figured out what colors to paint our walls, what our signs should look like, and what our retail areas look like. We found we had to be specific about our system because not everybody knew what to do. It's all about branding and who's better at branding than JP? You can't see a bottle of Paul Mitchell shampoo and not know what it is. Now when someone wants to open up a school, they need to follow our system, including the décor.

Winn has always supported the culture at JPMS, so it was a given that our culture would be a part of our Paul Mitchell Schools too. As we were building our first school, we had a number of brief daily meetings, often after a shot of Patrón, where we talked about all the details of the system. I'm a salesman. That's my talent. But Winn had fifteen years' of experience running a school by the time we put the first Paul Mitchell School together. He went through all the details with me, and I approved everything.

Depending on the school, we offer a lot of programs, from cosmetology to barbering to aesthetics. We also have shorter programs for nails and makeup. Our students—we call them future professionals—advance through different levels of training, becoming more confident as they move through each stage.

Showing We Care

Our students need to know that we care, and I make sure our schools know how much I support them. Winn and I appear at school grand openings. We give speeches, shake hands, and have our pictures taken with the hundreds of guests who show up. We have a big awards ceremony every year because people need to be acknowledged when they've done good. Winn and I stand on stage and give out awards for excellence in different areas like culture, leadership, education, curriculum, and on and on. And we do it every single year.

We've done huge seminars in Las Vegas just for our Paul Mitchell School future professionals, and we get a couple thousand. For those who might not be able to afford it, the school owners and JPMS run promotions for three months. We say, "Here's a bag full of Paul Mitchell products. You sell them and you come as our guest." These are students who've never been out of their home city, and we get them a flight to Las Vegas, feed them, house them, and give them a great educational show for a couple of days.

The beauty industry is such a great thing to be part of. Our future professionals are so diverse and come to our schools with so many different stories and backgrounds. It's impossible to describe the average student, because there is no such thing as average when it comes to the students in our schools. Some of them are fresh from high school and have known for years that they wanted to be stylists. Some come to us with college degrees or have left successful careers that they realized weren't what they wanted. Some have tried an assortment of things, and just not yet landed in the job that feels right. Being a hair stylist is, of course, a creative and artistic job, but it's also very technical, and it's social! A hair stylist not only cuts, colors, and styles hair – they help people feel great about themselves, boost self-esteem, put a smile on someone's face. A great haircut or color can make someone's day! It's such a satisfying career and can be so much fun! One of my granddaughters, Katie Mae, is currently attending one of our schools—she first did our aesthetician program, and now she's completing her hours to be a licensed make-up artist. I love that she is entering this field.

From Winn Claybaugh

John Paul is the real deal. To him leadership is about serving people. He truly has the heart of a servant, and that attitude shows up in our schools. He also encourages the people who work with him to serve others. When the schools started to take off and I was making even more money, he once pulled me aside and said, "I bet you're excited with extra money coming in. I bet you'd like to buy yourself a new expensive car."

I admitted he was right. I was going to buy myself a new car. Then he said, "Don't do it. Buy your mom a car instead." JP followed it up with, "You'll have plenty of time in your life to buy new incredible cars. But how much time will you have to buy your mom a fabulous car? By the way, don't buy her the type of car she always buys. Buy her the best car out there." So, I bought my mom a Mercedes. I get emotional when I think about it. I've shared that advice over and over since then.

Schools Giving Back

Of course, my favorite part of our school culture is about giving back. Every year each Paul Mitchell School does a three-month "FUNraising" campaign with a goal of raising fifteen thousand dollars. Some of them raise a lot more. They do anywhere from fifty to a hundred FUNraisers in that time. It might be something small like a bake sale or a car wash. Or it could be as big as a fashion show which they sell tickets to. The most important rule is that they not spend a lot of money to raise money. That means getting people to volunteer their services instead of paying for them. We want to make sure that all the money that's raised goes to helping someone.

From the start of our FUNraising in 2004 through the 2024 campaign, our Paul Mitchell Schools have raised over twenty-six million dollars. And by the way, those millions of dollars were not raised by receiving large, thousand-dollar donations but rather from five and ten dollar donations through the many grassroots events hosted by each school.

Winn and Me on stage revealing the check for Food for Africa, as a result of the FUNraising efforts

Photo courtesy of Winn Claybaugh

From Winn Claybaugh

Here's how our FUNraisers work. We usually choose between six and ten big charities. For example, Thirst Project, which works in the villages of eSwatini to build wells that provide clean, safe water—for life! Or the Gary Sinise Foundation, which builds mortgage-free, specially adapted smart homes for our most severely wounded heroes and provides funding for essential equipment and training to ensure our first responders can perform to the best of their abilities. Or Best Friends Animal Society, whose goal is to move more animals from shelters to homes and to make every shelter in America no-kill. Or Children's Miracle Network Hospitals, which pays for the treatment of twelve million children in 170 hospitals across the country each year. Or UNCF, which awards scholarships, supports historically Black colleges and universities, and serves as the nation's leading advocate for the importance of minority education and engagement. Or Food4Africa, which provides nutritional food to underprivileged children and orphans in South Africa. In 2005, John Paul invited us to raise money for Food4Africa. To date, funds raised by Paul Mitchell Schools have provided over thirty-five million meals through this wonderful organization.

We try to give to a variety of different charitable causes. We usually give checks for around one-hundred-thousand dollars to each charity.

I want to end this chapter with a quote from the Paul Mitchell Schools website. These are the core values our schools try to live up to:

1. Fostering the principles of fairness, equity, inclusion, anti-racism and social justice

2. Celebrating diversity, bringing out the best in people, and giving back locally and globally

3. Pursuing excellence in every aspect of a Paul Mitchell School education

Our vision is simple:

When people come first, success will follow.

Chapter 12

The Future of John Paul Mitchell Systems

We have over one hundred schools, and our products are sold in over 120 countries. Can you believe we're the #1 privately-owned, professional hairstyling brand worldwide today? That's wild. To top that off, we have a brilliant team that looks years ahead to ensure that JPMS is a company poised for long-term and sustained growth. They are evaluating or launching new innovations in product, education, processes, and always with the goal in mind to support the professional hairstylist industry. We're grounded in our principles as a company and are constantly looking ahead. We love what we do, and the future never stops feeling bright and exciting.

So, what is the future for John Paul Mitchell Systems? Two things will never change with the company—it will always be my baby and will always be somehow tied to the professional hairstylist industry. The reason John Paul Mitchell Systems is so important to me is twofold.

Number One: it's the first real business that I actually started on my own, other than small entrepreneurial things. I did it while homeless in my car. It became the world's largest privately owned professional haircare company. This really showed me how America works and what I could learn by being on the job, and learning while on the job, because I don't have a college degree.

Number Two: is that we told hairdressers we'd stay with and include them in what we do. We've always said, "If you support us, we won't do what all the other haircare companies have done. We won't sell our company to some big corporation. Our company won't disappear, and we will always in many ways support and include your industry." I will never ever go back on that, I told them. "Give us a chance," I said, and they believed me—they trusted me. And I will never go back on that promise.

While I was doing a presentation in 2004, a young hairdresser in the audience raised her hand and said, "Excuse me, Mr. DeJoria, but we know you've been offered a lot of money, many times, for your company. You haven't sold your company so we know you're honest. But what happens if you die?" I'd never thought of that before. What would the company do? What would my family do?

I sprang into action. First, I thanked this hairdresser for asking such a great question and spurring me to action. Then I went out and founded a 360-year trust in the United States. I put my holdings in that trust. It means that no matter what happens to me, the company can never be sold and must always stay connected to the professional beauty industry. No one can alter that, even as the industry changes. It was another way of saying, "Hey, I'm with you," to the hairdressers.

It was a promise to an industry that supported me when I had absolutely nothing and helped me build a multi-million-dollar company. That industry gave me the money to do all the rest I've been able to accomplish. For another 340-some-odd years, John Paul Mitchell Systems will remain in the professional beauty industry.

Young Michaeline & Me in a candid moment that ending up being one of the most iconic images of JPMS early years
Photo credit: Olof Wahlund

My daughter, Michaeline, is now CEO. When I'm long gone and no longer chairman, she'll take my job. But no one can break up the company. JPMS will stay whole, and her commitment is as solid as mine. She continues to adapt the company in a way that allows us to support hairdressers unwaveringly, and in step with how the industry and the world evolve. Further, we are so committed to our promise that in all those hundreds of years we still have to go, no other beneficiary or operator of the company could go against that principle.

Speaking of family commitment, Michaeline grew up in the industry and used to visit my office as a little girl. She knows every job because she has worked in every department in the company. She insisted on spending time working and learning in every department because she knew it would allow her to be the strongest leader possible one day. She has had a passion to run the company since she could speak and is committed to taking care of the company that has given our family so much, and the industry that helped us get there. Michaeline studied Product Development at the Fashion Institute of Design & Merchandising, as well as Organizational Communications and Industrial Psychology at Pepperdine University.

From Michaeline DeJoria

I used to go with my dad to the office. He was a single dad; my parents split before I was one year old. I never saw them together, but they were great friends who respected each other and got along very well. As a result, I had a very organic upbringing. If I missed one parent, I got to go there. If my dad was somewhere in the world that he or I thought would be a great experience for me, I got to be there. I was incredibly fortunate to not only see so much of the world, but to also have a front row view of him growing this incredible company, and all the companies after. It was an invaluable education that I never took for granted. Whenever I was with my dad and he would go to work, I always wanted to go to the office. From two years old, I would run around the office and answer the phones, fax things, write on people's papers. As I got older, I'd continue to find ways to help out and never stopped asking questions and trying to learn.

When I graduated college, I came to work at JPMS. I wasn't given a job and I wasn't paid. I just showed up and started doing things. I spent time in every single department, helping and asking questions. It helped me to understand even simple things. "So, this person hands you a PO, you write this and check on the computer, then you put it in the basket. Okay, got it." I wanted to learn everything I could about the business.

Eventually Luke (the then-President) asked if I wanted an official job. I was over the moon. When I first joined officially, I looked at all the departments, seeing how they could better integrate and make improvements. But it was important to me, before I ever got a title, that I spend time in every single department and learn it hands-on. If I wanted to be an effective leader one day, I needed to understand the implications of every decision on every level of the business.

My role in the company began to evolve from learning to observing to suggesting to implementing. I was on the board for several years before I stepped into my current role as CEO in 2021. In the years since, we've made profound changes in the business, but we will always maintain the same ethos. It's important that we hold on to those original pledges for the planet, for people, and especially for the professional hair care industry, as we innovate, evolve, and incorporate a new audience while holding on to our beloved loyal audience.

We have a hairdresser as President and he's one of the most brilliant in the world. Jason Yates is from the UK. He began his career over thirty years ago, starting as a salon apprentice, then a hairdresser, and working his way up to managing a group of twenty-two salons. He also worked as a platform artist and educated hairstylists for another hair care manufacturer. His diverse background made him a perfect fit for JPMS. Jason started out as our Vice President of Marketing and in 2021, began to oversee the daily global operations as President. He knows the hairdressing industry inside and out and is one of the sharpest guys on the planet.

From Jason Yates

I started as an apprentice hairdresser in a working-class town in the UK. I didn't have any education past high school, but I worked my way to a pretty high level behind the chair, then managed multiple salon locations, and finally got involved in the manufacturing side of the business as an educator. I was working for one of JP's competitors in the United States when one of our distributors (also the largest distributor of Paul Mitchell products in the world) told me that JP was looking for someone who understood the industry from a marketing capacity. I was aware of Paul Mitchell as a global mega brand and had seen JP at many events but never met him. My wife encouraged me to call, which led to an interview.

It was an eight-hour interview where I met all the key people in the company and they all spent time with me. I thought, "Wow, they really take their time and care about hiring." JP came and asked a few questions. I remember feeling a little intimidated. He's a billionaire, right? He's someone I admire but don't know that well. Then he asked a question that threw me. I don't even remember the question, but I remember my response. "You know, honestly, I don't have an answer."

He said, "Very good, young man. That shows me you have a lot of confidence to say in an interview that you don't know something."

That stuck with me. It was my first conversation with JP. And they offered me the job.

As soon as I walked into JPMS, I saw such a special aura around the whole company. It really comes from the legacy of JP and Paul Mitchell. You can tell that when JP and Paul got together, something magical happened. Their magic was still very much alive and still is today. It may sound corny, but as soon as I walked through the doors as an employee, I felt a sense of pride and love. Everybody really respected each other.

In 2012, I started off at the company as Vice President of global marketing. Things went well and JPMS was heading on a good trajectory. I felt I understood other areas of the company and had good relationships. In 2015, after interviewing several people, JP and Luke asked me to take on the added responsibility of sales and marketing. It was the first time in the history of JPMS they'd given those two jobs to one person. The deeper connection went well, because it's everything we try to do in business—sales and marketing. When Luke was getting closer to retirement, they also wanted me to take on more responsibility. First, it was education, then making the creative department digital. In 2017, JP made me chief operations officer and they handed me everything else. Then in 2021, JP promoted me to President and Michaeline to CEO. She and I kind of went through that eight-year journey together. It was almost like JP had this grand master plan. Just as Luke and JP had played those roles for the last thirty years, he was looking to create that same kind of dynamic between Michaeline and me. And we have been working beautifully together. In the past few years, our work has really started to pay dividends.

John Paul cares about people more than he cares about himself, and he cares deeply about hairdressers. The fact that I'm a hairdresser and President of JPMS today supports that. Nobody else would have ever put me in charge of their company, because I finished my formal education at 15. I do have a lot of experience, but it's all hands-on. JP can relate though, because he was a self-made man. He had to work after high school. He had to hustle. We're alike in that way. I saw that soon after joined the company. I'm such a workaholic. The hardest thing for me to do is to relax. And JP is always on the go so I know I'm in good company!

So, we have two nice young people running things, although I'm still the Chairman of the Board. It's funny, when I started the company, our average age was late thirties to early forties. The same people are still alive, and many are working at JPMS, but our staff now, when you take me out of it, averages about the same age as Paul and I were over forty years ago.

Chapter 13

My Business Back Bar

People ask me these questions over and over again: How do I make business decisions? How do I manage a business? How do I think? Not much has changed. Many of the things I did when I started JPMS I still do today. I believed back then it's important to treat people right and I still do, whether they're working for me or struggling with homelessness. I always ask myself first, how would I like to be treated? It's served me pretty well over the years. Now that I've made that clear, here's some of my thinking on those questions I seem to get asked a lot.

On Hiring

Hiring people is something I do from the heart. I want to know how I feel and not just about your resume. Anybody can fill out a resume. How do I feel about you? How do I feel about the person who's talking to me? How do I feel about the back-and-forth energy we have? Are you enthusiastic? Can you look me in the eye? Do I feel good about you? Are you looking for a future or just a job for now? What do you want to be doing in five or ten years? I get that by talking to people. If I get a good feeling, we give it a try. I admit I'm not right every time, probably ninety percent of the time. That's a pretty good batting average. But ten percent of the time I miss the mark. If it turns out I'm not right and I don't fire that person or let them go, I'm doing more of an injustice to them than to myself. If someone just takes a job for the money, but isn't doing something that touches their heart, I need to let them go so they have an opportunity to search for their sweet spot in life.

On Management

None of my companies—not Paul Mitchell, not Patrón, nor any of the new ones—have what the corporate world calls middle management. I want to hire people who are good enough at their jobs that they don't need a supervisor supervising them, or a Vice President supervising a bunch of supervisors to check in on what they're doing. There's no need for layers of management if you get people trained well enough to perform at optimum levels in their jobs. You only need one or two persons between them, let's say the President or CEO.

From Luke Jacobellis

JP has always believed that there are too many middlemen in business. That's one of the reasons he was fired years ago. He just doesn't see the need to have all those extra people around. He and I would always question ourselves whenever the topic of a new hire came up. We would always ask: Is there a better way? Could Susie or Fred pick up stuff? Until about eight years ago, we didn't even have an HR department. And we never had a problem. That's because we treated people well. Plus, JP always paid very well so we retained people. A lot of other companies have enormous training and retraining costs because of their turnover.

Learn at Each Step

Don't go out there and think you're going to have a billion-dollar business the first year (unless you're really, *really* lucky). You need to get an education first, go through all the ups and downs, and learn what worked and what didn't work. When you get rid of what doesn't work, you can capitalize on what does work. So, I say to everyone out there, be patient and learn how to run what you're doing perfectly before taking the next step up. That's what we did to grow.

Learning how to manage people is a great example. It's easy when there are only one or two employees. What about when you have a hundred? I remember when Luke Jacobellis started to work for us. He came as a consultant and ended up reorganizing our warehouse. I wasn't a warehouse expert, but I could see how his input was helping the business.

One day, the woman who'd been handling the warehouse came to me and said, "I don't like what Luke is doing here. So, I'm going to tell you this. It's either him or me."

I said to her in the kindest way, "But you reached your limit. He can take us further along."

"Well, I'm leaving then," she answered.

I told her, "I'm sorry about that. I'll give you a nice severance pay."

I learned how important it was to have good people working for you. I also learned that some people think they are better than they actually are or don't recognize that they have stopped growing and therefore reached their capacity. Recognizing those situations is all part of leadership. You have to deal with people's egos, and in my case, I want to make everybody happy. I have learned over the years how to make the right decisions for my companies and for the people who work for me. It's a balancing act.

In my warehouse example, I had a choice to make. When there is someone out there who can do the job better and someone on the team can't (or won't) take advice from them or learn from them how to be better, then they may as well get off the bus. If the woman hadn't given me an ultimatum, she would still have had a job with me. Sadly, learning from Luke would have made her a lot smarter.

On Reprimanding and Praising

Many employees are very upset when they are reprimanded. There is a way to reprimand so that when they walk out, they feel really good about themselves. Have these three points ready before you bring them in.

1. Tell them what the challenge is so they can understand it. (don't call it a problem).

2. Explain to them why you want it done differently and how it affects everyone.

3. Be sure to let them know what they are doing really well right now, and before they leave, give an example. The example is, "John, you are one of the best

presenters we have. You do a great job there, so I know it will be easy for you to solve the challenge." Leave people with dignity and self-worth and they leave liking the person they talked to.

On Praise: Praise people loudly and in front of as many people as you can!

On Living Within Your Means

There's an old saying that I love: If you expect change, don't do things the same way.

I say the same thing about finance. If you have a good year, pretend it's the last year you'll ever make that kind of money. Don't change your standard of living for a year. A lot of people in the entertainment industry live like millionaires, then lose everything because they had a one-hit wonder. If you are going to change your lifestyle, make sure you have at least six months of living expenses in the bank. And don't take on any new bills yet, unless it's for a mortgage, and try to keep that low. If you never spend more than one-third of your income on rent or a mortgage, you'll have a much better chance to make it.

On Prioritizing

I usually have a whole bunch of things to do every day. So, I prioritize. I ask myself, what's the most important thing right now and I try to do that first. If the people I need to call live in different time zones, I prioritize based on the best time to reach them. If I don't reach them, I keep calling back until I finally get hold of them. I also think about what's the most important thing tomorrow or next week. If something is really important, and something else might get in the way, I change the date on the less important thing.

I have a lot of investments and charities I give to. My motto is to pay attention to the vital few and ignore the trivial many. I believe in hiring experts to help me. It's important to build people around you that either know more than you about something or are better at doing something than you are. It even works on a small scale. That's how you get to a bigger scale.

On Research

It should be no surprise I do research on things I'm thinking about getting involved with or investing money in. I have a team in Austin, Texas who are brilliant in so many areas: with different types of energy, real estate, and a variety of things. I go to them and ask, "What do you think of this business? Does it make sense for me?" Sometimes I want to see things myself, so I'll have the person asking me to invest to send samples of their work or their product. I give them to my home office people to look at and evaluate. I'll ask, "What is this?" "Is it real?" "Will it work?" "Will it make a difference?" That's how I do the due diligence.

I'm looking for, "Yeah, this is good," or "This is bad for you." That's how we get involved (or not). I'm smart enough to know that I'm not good about some things—and I'm not stupid! I'm uninformed in so many areas that I've got to go to someone who really knows. Their feedback and advice contributes to how I make decisions. I'm pretty right on maybe eighty to ninety percent of the time because of my due diligence. Occasionally a bad idea will slip through, but not most of the time.

On Keeping a Home Office

I have a home office that kind of runs my businesses. These people make sure my money comes in when it's supposed to and goes out when it's supposed to. When needed, we bring in other people to check on existing businesses to see how well they're doing. If something is amiss, I know immediately, and it allows me to take action. For example, one business was requiring more money than it should for the return we expected. They shut that down for me immediately. I've invested in forty or fifty businesses over the years. Crazy. As you would expect, a few of them were deadbeats that weren't going anywhere, and they got them off my sheet. I probably meet with my manager once every week or two over coffee and spend an hour or so going over things.

It is imperative to have a team of people you trust and who have the talent to do what you need done. I keep a list of my own by writing everything down. I check it on a monthly basis to make sure the people I'm working with are following through—and that I'm following through too!

On Making Investment Decisions

There are a lot of steps to making a good investment decision. If something comes up that excites me to get involved in or expand with, I first look to see if it touches me in the heart.

Of course, it needs to make sense in my brain too, but how my heart responds is more important. Does it feel good? Am I moved to do it? After that, I work out the math. If I put in so much money to do this, what will the return be? And the top priority for me is: Will it make a difference, and will it help people out?

It's exceedingly important to know who I can get to work with me on new business ventures—especially if it's an area I know little about. I may understand the business part but not the technical part or the technical terminology of the business. I make sure there's someone with me who knows what the hell they're doing. If I can't do it right and for the right reasons, why spin my wheels?

Then I ask myself if I'm happy with the people in this industry and happy to be around them. It's a combination of happiness and how my heart feels about it. I want a darned good partner who can be trusted as well as someone who knows what he's doing. When I find the right person, I give them an incentive to *really* want to do it. If they don't do it, there are incentives for that too. If it turns out we're both wrong and it doesn't work out, I still give a good recommendation so they can go on to their next best thing.

On Business Failures as Learning Experiences

You already know by now that not everything I've done has turned into a success. You can't win them all. I try to learn from everything I get involved in. But, boy, have I made some big mistakes. Most of them have been because I didn't know what I was doing when I got into a business. I've been blessed with being right probably ninety percent of the time, but it's that other ten percent that gives you an education you never forget.

I wanted to go into the telephone business back in 1989. I thought I'd make a fortune selling minutes. I bought time from a major phone company to sell to customers, figuring I'd make a profit. The way it worked is this: let's say I paid one cent a minute for the time. I'd turn around and sell it for twenty cents a minute to people who had cellular phones, right? I bought this company to do just that, and I put a lot of money into it. As I started the business, prices on cellular phones started coming down instead of going up as I'd figured they would. On our end, prices per minute increased but they were going down at the other end. It turned out the margins were so small that the resale business kind of went away. I lost out on that one and it was a pretty good-sized loss.

I once was a major investor in a business with Wolfgang Puck, one of the most successful chefs in the world. It was a restaurant and brewery in West Los Angeles called Eureka, one of the first combination restaurants and breweries ever put together. From the day we opened the doors, the restaurant was full for lunch and dinner. But the bigger part of our investment was the brewery. We had unbelievably beautiful copper stills and it cost more money for the distillery than it did for the restaurant The problem was that Wolfgang and I didn't know anything about brewing beer! We'd hired this young guy to help with that part, but it wasn't enough. Even though the restaurant stayed full, within one year we lost a lot of money because we didn't know what the hell we were doing. We closed it and declared bankruptcy. We learned that Wolfgang did great restaurants and I did great promotions, but neither one of us was good at running a brewery. We both learned enough that we never made that mistake again. I don't think Wolfgang ever lost a restaurant again. This one failed because we thought beer would be easy. Nope.

On Giving Gratitude

Before I go to bed at night, I always give gratitude. I try to cover all possibilities, so I give my gratitude to the "creator of souls." I say thank you for this incredibly healthy life you've given me. I really appreciate it. I hope I always do good with it because I know that I'm the active presence of the creator in me. Then I go to bed with a clear mind. If I wake up at night thinking about something, I write it down on a piece of paper, set it aside, and go back to sleep. That way I don't have to think about it until I get up in the morning.

Chapter 14
Patrón

Sometimes a business decision can lead to great success even if you don't know what you're doing at first. The key is to be patient, persistent, and, as I said earlier, find the right people to run it. That's what happened with Patrón, and I couldn't be happier. Without Patrón, I could not have done nearly as much as I have to change the world.

Back in the 1980s, my friends and I loved tequila. It was cheap and made a perfect mixer for a lot of drinks. But we wanted to see if we could find a better tequila. When my buddy, Martin Crowley, made a business trip to Mexico I asked him to bring back some really good tequila. What he brought back was amazing. It came packaged in a plain glass bottle but it was different from all the other tequilas. (Later, we designed our own recycled, hand-blown glass bottle.) I thought, why not make our own version and sell it in the United States? Of course, neither of us knew the first thing about making tequila or selling spirits. But that didn't stop us. We figured if it didn't sell, that was cool. We'd give it away as gifts to our friends and family.

We booked a flight to Mexico where we met with Francisco Alcaraz, a chemical engineer. To make the smoother, quality kind of tequila we were looking for, Alcaraz told us that it should be made at a certain distillery, because they had the equipment to make it in the old school way. The method took more time but the quality of the tequila would be better. We agreed and made Francisco our master distiller. Our first twelve thousand bottles of Patrón hit the market in 1989 selling for thirty-seven dollars.

It was the same year that Paul Mitchell passed away. Needless to say, a great deal of my attention was on JPMS during that time.

I got creative with my time and my methods to promote my fledgling brand of tequila. I would spend my evenings carrying around bottles of Patrón to bars and restaurants.

I would go into a bar and say to the bartender, "I'd like to buy you a shot of your best tequila." They'd pour their favorite and drink it.

Then I'd say, "May I have an empty glass?" After they put one on the bar, I'd reach into my briefcase and pull out a bottle of Patrón and pour a generous shot. "Now try this."

They'd drink it and without exception, the reaction was always, "Wow! What is that?"

With a broad grin on my face, I would answer, "That's the new world of tequila. It's called Patrón and we're just introducing this ultra-premium tequila to the United States."

And that's how we started out.

After we got it going in a few places we looked for a distributor. At first, they all laughed at us. They would tell me, "There's no market for quality tequila at your price in the United States." Undeterred, we kept pursuing and it took us a while to find a distributor willing to work with us. The first one only sold 1,200 cases the first year. Our second distributor, Jim Beam, agreed it was the best tequila but too pricey. They said we would never sell more than 20,000 cases a year (they were selling 12,000 cases a year at the time).

We needed to sell a lot more if we were going to make any money.

But we stuck it out and expanded our marketing to different audiences. I'd go to our major Paul Mitchell seminars with 3,000 salon owners and hair stylists in attendance and serve them all free Patrón at the last night party. And we'd give them two tickets to redeem at the bar. Afterwards, they'd go home and ask their liquor stores for it because it was that good.

We ended up going to Seagram's as our distributor and they took it up to around 40,000 cases a year. When Patrón started doing better, Seagram's decided to build their own distillery to make it. Martin and I wanted out of our contract with them because they were going to use more modern techniques. We knew that the Seagram's distillery wouldn't be able to recreate our Patrón tequila with their methods and we wound up buying them out of their agreement.

It was around that time that Ed Brown came into the picture. His dad was in the liquor business. During his time working at Seagram's, he got to know us. In 2000, when we were looking for an Executive Vice President, he agreed to take on the job. Later, he became our Chief Executive Officer, one of the best decisions we ever made for Patrón.

From Ed Brown

I was working for Seagram's when I first met Martin and John Paul. Neither one of them knew much about the alcohol business and they called me quite often. I was in China when they asked me to come talk to them about running their business. When I met them, we had a great conversation and I said, "Hey listen, make me an offer I can't refuse." They had a pretty good offer back to me in about an hour, and I said, "Sure, I'll do this." When I told my best friend, who also worked for Seagram's that I was going to work for Patrón, he said I was going to be the laughing stock of the industry.

Four months later, Martin called and said he wanted to sell the business. I'm thinking, now what am I going to do? But before I could sell the business, I got another call that Martin had passed away. So, I called JP and told him I didn't think he should sell the business. JP suggested we have a conversation. At breakfast the next day I said, "I just think this brand has a lot of potential that you guys haven't even tapped. It would be a shame to sell the business without really giving it a try."

JP agreed not to sell it. Then I told him I wanted to be his partner in the business. JP said, "Done deal. What else do you want to talk about?" I told him that there may come a day when we should sell and I'd let him know when it was time. We agreed to go in together as partners, and when the time did come, he kept his word.

With Ed Brown at the helm, the Patrón business skyrocketed. Oh my God, there was no end in sight. We went beyond what anyone ever imagined.

First of all, we were building our own distillery. Francisco would work for us full-time as our Master Distiller. There was nothing wrong with our third-party manufacturer, except that our margins were terrible, and it seemed they couldn't increase production. Ed felt he could get Patrón profits up much higher with increased production capabilities.

We didn't own any agave farms. It made no sense for us to do that. Agave is a commodity, and the price goes up and down depending on the crops. Nature would have controlled how much Patrón we could make from year to year. Instead, we had contracts with about twenty good farms, and we paid them immediately. We also sometimes paid them more than the other tequila companies. Paying immediately and paying more is the tactic that served us well. For the growers, the way we treated them was a big deal, and they were very loyal to us over the years. Also, we wouldn't buy or use agave that was younger than six years old. We usually bought it at the seven- or eight-year mark. The longer you grow it, the better it is. It's also more expensive, of course, but that's what made it the best.

From Ed Brown

I was always very strict, even religious, about how Patrón was made. Our tequila had to be unbelievable, because you can't outsmart today's consumer. It's not just the liquid that has to be good or the package or even you. It's the whole story. I didn't care how much it cost to make. I wanted to make sure we were making the best juice.

Most people wouldn't have done what we did at the distillery. Our agave was cut by hand, and we used brick ovens. Our pot stills were handmade, and we still used the old tahona culture to crush the agave. The tahona is a big lava rock that weighs tons. It crushes the agave to squeeze the juice out. In the old days they used mules to pull the tahona wheel, but we automated that process by using a robot. It was a slow and expensive way to do what we did, but it was the best way to make tequila. We believe the tahona gives nuances to the brand and a different taste.

The method most places still use is called a roller mill. It's like a big shredder which is cheaper because it's quick and more efficient. But it doesn't produce the best tequila.

When our business grew and we needed to produce more, we didn't try to mass-produce the tequila like everyone else. We simply replicated our small distillery hundreds of times. Each micro distillery inside our building was responsible for making only a specific number of cases (say ten thousand) a year. That's how I made sure that our quality was always perfect. That first distillery was about thirty thousand square feet. The size now is probably about two million square feet.

The second move we made was to change our marketing. We had the finest product on the market, and it came in a bottle that was unique. The package was eye-catching and so different from the other tequila bottles. Also, it was sold in a box with tissue paper which made it look like a gift. Patrón was a quality product and most everyone who bought it wanted to reorder. So, what could we do to make our sales go up?

The problem was that we were focusing on placing ads with beautiful, sexy women in magazines like *Playboy*. This limited our audience. Ed suggested if we wanted better sales, we needed to go after a wider marketplace. Then he came up with a great slogan which we added to our bottles. He said it came to him in the middle of the night so he wrote it down on a notepad. It was "Simply Perfect." Brilliant! He changed the ads for Patrón to show a picture of the bottle with "Simply Perfect" printed below. One more thing: Because he had worked for Seagram's, Ed also had great connections with lots of distributors, especially Southern Wine and Spirits, and they made a big difference. Patrón started to sell everywhere.

From Ed Brown

We built our distillery in record time but all we had was silver tequila. We didn't have any brown tequila like reposado or añejo because it has to age. So, I told my distributors that I'm just selling silver tequila for the next year and a half. They complained that nobody drinks silver tequila, and I said, "We're going to prove to people that Patrón Silver is the most mixable drink in the world." I also told them I didn't want to be just in Mexican restaurants. I wanted our high premium spirit to be in every nightclub and high-end restaurant—every place that's got energy and young people.

Six months later, we were selling as much as the best-selling vodka. Today Patrón Silver is the largest selling brand by itself. It does 3.1 million cases. At the time we sold, Patrón had a ninety percent market share.

Thanks to Ed Brown, we still had a quality tequila, a great ad, and a new approach to marketing. We worked together to build Patrón. JPMS was in good shape, so I was able to spend more time selling tequila. I worked hard to get it out into the world by doing whatever Ed needed. People were used to my being on television, talking about Paul Mitchell, and I did the same for Patrón. If he needed me to go to an event and talk, I was on it. Ed always said he did the preparation work, and he would put me in the press to talk about the product. My favorite job!

Ed Brown and Me at the Patrón Hacienda
Photo courtesy of author's personal collection

Then, a few things happened that pumped up Patrón's image as a hip spirit. Some rappers started talking about it. Clint Eastwood is a buddy of mine. One day, he called me and said, "JP, I just put this movie up, *In the Line of Fire*, and I want to invite you and Eloise to come see the premiere. There's something in it you're going to like." We went to the premiere to watch the movie, and there it was, a bottle of Patrón! Nobody asked him to do it. He just put the bottle there on his own.

From Ed Brown

I built our distillery to look like an 1820 old hacienda and it was beautiful. While we were building, John Paul never saw it because I wanted to complete everything in Mexico first. When I finally showed him the place two years later, he couldn't speak. I opened the doors and he said, "How much did this cost us?" Then he said, "Don't tell me. I don't want to know. Don't ever tell me. It's so amazing and beautiful. I don't want it to be ruined by the cost." To this day, he has no idea how much it cost. It wasn't as bad as he probably imagined because we built it in Mexico.

JP is my favorite man. I was just a kid when I started working with him. Sure, I would have had a nice career with Seagram's. But to have somebody who would become not just my best friend but my partner and trust me in the way he did was the best. We have such a unique relationship even today. My dad died when I was thirty and JP became like a father, mentor and best friend to me.

One day in 2018, Ed came to me and said, "It's time to sell."

My reply was, "I don't need to sell."

"JP, if you were okay to sell, how much would you want?"

My answer was "I'd like to have a valuation over five billion dollars."

Ed came back with, "JP, are you aware that the biggest brand in the industry sold for approximately 2.2 billion dollars?"

"Patrón is much more valuable and I don't need to sell."

Ed came back a short time later and said, "JP, we have a 5.1 billion dollar valuation on the company."

As majority shareholder, the answer was "Yes!"

You know, I give a lot of speeches and I talk about leadership. What makes great leaders? Great leaders know what they know. That's why I asked for 5.1 billion dollar valuation. But leaders also know what they *don't* know even better. It's why they surround themselves with people who can fill in those gaps—people like Ed Brown.

It took a few months, but we ended up selling Patrón to Bacardi for a very good valuation. So, Ed and I, along with Bacardi, put a generous portion of our proceeds into a pool for all the Patrón employees. Without them, we would never have gotten where we did.

SUCCESS UNSHARED IS FAILURE

Chapter 15

JP's Peace, Love & Happiness Family Foundation

I've been blessed. The lifestyle I live now is beyond what I ever could have imagined all those years ago when I was homeless and trying to make a couple of bucks to cover a day's worth of meals for me and my young son. But my mom taught me the importance of caring, giving, and finding a little something extra to give to someone in need, even when it seemed we didn't have enough. That's something I've carried with me all my life.

People were always there for me when I needed a helping hand. It's wonderful now to be able to make such a big difference in the lives of others with the money I have. It's also true that you don't need money to make a difference in the world. I've met so many people who have next to nothing and still find ways to give. Back in my heavy-duty biker years when I didn't have any money, they had a kind of Thanksgiving at Christmas at Griffith Park in Los Angeles. People would donate food, and they would serve a full meal to each of the hundreds of people who came. I felt like doing something to give back, so I went down there and volunteered to help serve food and clean up afterwards.

Here's another example. When we do events with nonprofits across the United States, we invite students from

Paul Mitchell Schools or hairdressers from our salons to do people's hair. They make people look and feel better while raising money or bringing attention to a cause. People can give back by taking time to do something for somebody else, something that needs to be done, like mowing a lawn for an elderly neighbor. You can make a huge difference in people's lives, and it costs you absolutely nothing to do it. Every time you do things out of your own heart to help others, it expands your heart.

As I have always said, giving without expecting anything in return is the greatest high, the greatest feeling. When I'm giving, I feel worthy of being here, like it's my way of paying rent for being on this planet Earth!

Creating Partnerships that Last

While I used to respond to requests as they came in, I now have a person who brings me grant proposals. Constance Dykhuizen is the executive director of JP's Peace, Love & Happiness Family Foundation, the private family foundation that handles all personal philanthropy for Eloise and me. Constance was my son's babysitter when he was little and she was in graduate school. Whenever we'd come home from an event, she was always studying, so I knew she took her work seriously.

From Constance Dykhuizen

When I finished graduate school, I wanted to work overseas, so I asked John Paul where I could be of help. I moved to Thailand and worked for an NGO that his Southeast Asia distributor founded to prevent trafficking of school-age kids. I learned so much about what nonprofits need and how donors can help them. When I moved back to the U.S. in 2011, I suggested to John Paul that he start a foundation to formalize his giving, since he'd just signed the Giving Pledge. He had already been considering it and had the name ready to go—JP's Peace, Love & Happiness Family Foundation. Our mission is to contribute to a sustainable planet through investing in people, protecting animals and conserving the environment.

Of course, John Paul was philanthropic before we started the foundation. A lot of his charitable giving is driven by experiences he's had himself of being homeless, experiencing food insecurity and being a veteran. That interest in meeting felt needs, needs he himself has experienced, also makes him great at connecting with our partners. We are lucky to work with so many hard-working and compassionate people who are leaders in their communities and usually have lived experience or a personal connection to the work. These are the types of people we seek to invest in.

As a private family foundation, we don't accept unsolicited requests, but we work to make sure we are building relationships with local and global organizations that are aligned with the experiences and priorities of the DeJoria family. John Paul is absolutely delighted to meet the folks we are helping, and he genuinely connects with them. At Mobile Loaves & Fishes, he loves to visit the artists and see their latest pieces. At our first big event in Kentucky with Grow Appalachia, John Paul hopped on a nearby tractor in a field because wanted to see how it worked. I think it made everyone nervous—can this guy handle it? Of course he could. His curiosity and friendliness immediately disarm people when they realize he's himself, not what they think of when they think of a billionaire. At that same event in Kentucky, he stood for hours as people brought gifts – baskets of canned vegetables, a homemade quilt, even a jar of moonshine – as symbols of gratitude for funding their backyard gardens. He graciously accepted each gift and shook hands or hugged each person before leaving. That's who he is.

———— ✻ ————

Me and Constance Dykhuizen, Executive Director of JP's Peace, Love & Happiness Family Foundation
Photo courtesy of JP's Peace, Love & Happiness Family Foundation

Let's say of ten requests brought to me, maybe one will make sense and appeal to me and the heart level where I know it will truly make a difference. I like to help people who have experience with a special need or show a commitment to filling one. When presented with a request, I look at its purpose and try to see how I can help. Mobile Loaves & Fishes is a great example. It started out feeding unhoused people and is now a first-of-its-kind tiny home community. I know what being homeless is like; I can relate to not having enough food or living out of your car. That meant something to me to meet those needs for others.

Many veterans are suffering from injuries or invisible wounds of PTSD. I have a lot of respect for these men and women because I served in the military. When I heard about Kathryn Chandler's vision for Patriots' Hall in Dripping Springs, I knew I wanted to support a place like that. It's a beautiful retreat and resource center in Central Texas. Texas has the highest number of veterans in the U.S., and the area between Killeen and San Antonio has the highest concentration. Patriots' Hall is a place for veterans and their families to gather and get help with VA claims or hold meetings or even work out in community. I am so glad I've been able to be a part of this resource for vets. Too often, they are forgotten.

From Constance Dykhuizen

When I've worked with an organization to figure out their needs and we have a project proposal, John Paul immediately wants to go visit them. He wants to shake hands, walk around the building site or the community center and figure out how he can help solve problems that they are experiencing. I think people are most surprised by his energy and approachability when they meet him. He always asks questions and wants to know how quickly they can get it done. Once we approve a project, he gives them funding, and then he trusts them to do it. We can't meet every need, but the best part of my job is being able to make connections for John Paul and Eloise that go on to transform lives.

During COVID, I really wanted to do something to help protect the homeless, so I contacted Dell Medical School at The University of Texas and offered to fund testing and medical care on the streets. During that time, Eloise and I worked with our personal chef to make and serve meals to medical personnel and first responders. We showed up and helped prep and deliver thousands of meals, all healthy and delicious. When I saw how responsive they were, I committed to endow JP's Peace, Love & Happiness Family Foundation Chair at the Department of Population Health which is focused on medical care for the unhoused. The team provides care right where they live, on the streets and in camps. This endowment will live on forever, with someone always thinking about what can be done and how to best provide services for the homeless.

That's the way it works. One thing leads to another, and another, and everything enhances what comes before it. I get a lot of people coming straight to me for help, but that's not how I work. We develop relationships, work together to make a plan and they have to prove that they're committed. The process is to go through Constance and my foundation if they want me to take them seriously.

———— ❊ ————

From Constance Dykhuizen

I can't emphasize how vital Eloise is to the foundation. If we go to a shelter for trafficking victims, she'll show up, be present, and offer to clean out her closet to donate what they can use. She has a heart for people and for women especially. She was an actress, so she loves to sponsor young creatives and film festivals. JP and Eloise each have their own interests, but they always support each other.

———— ❊ ————

It's important for me to tell you how much my wife Eloise contributes to the foundation. She stands by me at every opening and charity event. She supports all of my giving and connects me to good causes she thinks I ought to know about. Eloise also has her own causes that we give to as well.

Eloise and Me at Grow Appalachia
Photo credit: Ariana Jordan

———— ✳ ————

From Eloise

I grew up in a different world from John Paul. My mother was an artist and she worked with oils. I remember watching her work all day long creating this amazing art. Supporting the arts is hugely important to me because it connects me with my mother. I also worked as an actress for a short time before marrying John Paul, so I try to help the film community. If the subject of a film is about the environment or something that's important to JP, I let him know about it. Constance often finds short films that are looking for producers. "More Than I Want to Remember" is about a woman's experience coming in as an immigrant. It was a small project that ended up winning a lot of awards. I have also been proud to present the ConnectHER Film Festival for the last decade which encourages young filmmakers around the world to submit short films about issues that impact women and girls. We get to award these young people and encourage them in their art.

Protecting women is another concern for me. I was very lost when I was young and had a relationship with someone that was not great. That's probably why helping abused women makes me feel good. We support SAFE in Austin, which stands for "Stop Abuse for Everyone." Through them we funded Eloise House, where anyone can get forensic testing done in case of sexual assault.

———— ✳ ————

Getting People What They Need

Whether it's in the United States or across the oceans, there are hungry people wherever you go. The investments I make through JP's Peace, Love & Happiness Family Foundation don't make a monetary return; it's a way to build people up so they can invest in themselves. I do a lot to help the homeless and the hungry, but it's the people I meet that give me hope. Lisa's one of the more impressive people I've met, and she was working for a food rescue organization with little help and even less money. Not anymore.

Keep Austin Fed

Constance came to me one day and said, "JP, you've got to meet Lisa from Keep Austin Fed. She rescues food."

I found Lisa to be a delight. She is the sweetest lady in the world. She was going around to restaurants, sandwich shops and grocery stores collecting unsold produce and prepared food, knowing that it would otherwise get thrown out, and getting it to people who needed it.

I was impressed. "Oh my God, how many people work for you?"

She answered, "Besides volunteers, it's just me. We can't afford any staff yet. I work full time for our charity and do this."

I was shocked. "What? Well times are going to change."

From Lisa Barden

When the call came to confirm my meeting with John Paul, I was told it would be that day in twenty minutes. It was a weekend and I was out for breakfast with some friends. I ran home, changed out of my sweats, and tried to make myself presentable.

Then I met him at a bar in East Austin along with his team and my volunteer who'd told me about him. I had some trepidation going into this meeting, being totally unprepared and having to pivot to my professional face on a weekend. But JP made me feel welcome and put me at ease.

The first thing he did was offer me a margarita and we chatted for a bit. It was like he really wanted to get to know us. After asking how much more we needed to raise to make our budget for the year, he said, "If I give you the rest, you can focus on your programming. Will that work for you?"

It was the best meeting ever with a philanthropist or foundation. There was no long application to fill out. It was just a conversation between our organization and John Paul. And he liked us. He liked what we were doing. A couple of months later COVID hit and lots of organizations had to shut down. We were constantly juggling to find food and the need had gotten worse. It was really nice to have already secured that funding and not to have to apply for grants. Our work continued.

Today, Keep Austin Fed has more than one hundred sixty active volunteers who do over seven hundred food runs every month to food pantries, homeless shelters, even affordable housing complexes. They also do over a dozen grocery giveaways every week where they go straight to communities with needs and set up tables in common areas with boxes full of food.

In 2010, the USDA estimated the amount of food loss and waste from the food supply at the retail and consumer levels was about thirty-one percent. By rescuing thousands of meals every month and keeping hundreds of people fed, the organization is putting a dent in the amount of food in the U.S. that ends up in a landfill and produces harmful methane gas. It's a win-win.

From Lisa Barden

JP has helped us in so many ways. We have enough money to hire a staff of four besides me. He also gave us the funds to build an outdoor walk-in cooler where we're able to store food, because a lot of our partner organizations close early and food can't be delivered until the following day. We call it our East Austin hub. He also provided the funding for us to purchase a van to use for our giveaway events.

JP makes it easy for us to get money when we need it. If he likes what you're doing, he funds it. He trusts the organizations he funds, because he checks them out himself before he gives any money. He also volunteers with a lot of those organizations. He's boots on the ground and will even help hand out meals at homeless encampments. We try not to lean on him. In 2021, in fact, we didn't take any money from him. We told him to give it to another organization that wasn't having the luck we were having.

Can you believe it? She told me to give the money to someone else, because they were doing okay. That's a lady with a big heart who saw a way to do some good. Of course, I want to jump in and embrace her. People like Lisa show us how anyone can make a big difference in the world. Even if they don't have money or a lot of extra time to give.

Grow Appalachia

When I heard Tommy Callahan, a friend of mine and a Senior Vice President at JPMS, talk about growing up in Appalachia and how people were still experiencing hunger and food insecurity there, I decided to do something about it. It was around 2009, and the area was still impacted by the coal mines closing. The government made all these promises to help but it didn't reach to the people who needed it. I said, "Let's get these people fed. Let's put them in business."

I believe in empowering people to help themselves, so in cooperation with Berea College in Kentucky, I financed a program we created called Grow Appalachia. It teaches people in this region how to grow food and some people go on to make money from it as well. It was a small project to start and expanded to include all the states in the region. Grow Appalachia is now the largest program of its kind in the United States.

I asked for volunteers and paid for some staff, which included David Cooke as co-founder and our first director. We worked with people who were unemployed to help them grow their own gardens to feed themselves. Our plan was to address the specific needs of the individuals and families we worked with. Some only needed help with tillage and fertilization. Others were starting from scratch. We tried to provide each household with whatever was necessary to succeed.

We paid for seeds, fertilizer, and tillers and encouraged people to grow organically. Berea College did the training and I provided money. We developed a curriculum with things like canning classes that had materials all provided so that people had something to eat in the winter when their gardens weren't growing. That was phase one and the first year—getting started and feeding families.

David Cooke, Eloise, Me, and Candace Mullins at Grow Appalachia
Photo credit: Ariana Jordan

In phase two, we showed people how to grow a bit more food and sell the extra produce to farmers markets or local grocery stores. Now they were in business. We also taught them how to market, making sure they understood the importance of telling people they had organically grown, local produce. Since its founding, Grow Appalachia has partnered with families and small farmers to produce 7.3 million pounds of food that has an estimated economic value of more than eighteen million dollars. Giving can literally multiply when you get good people to help out. Berea College, a private liberal arts work college and our partner, was the first integrated co-educational college in the South and anybody in the region can attend at no cost. No student at Berea has had to pay tuition since 1892. How about that for a great partner!

**Me driving a tractor while helping to plant a farm in Kentucky
with Grow Appalachia**

Mobile Loaves & Fishes

Shortly after Grow Appalachia started, I got involved in a project closer to home called Mobile Loaves & Fishes. It was originally a food truck ministry started in Austin in 1998 by Alan Graham to feed the homeless. When I first pulled up to their little model RV home, I had no idea that we were about to change how Austin, and people all over the world, help the homeless.

From Alan Graham

I was in the real estate business most of my adult life but going on a men's retreat in 1996 had an extraordinary impact on me. I'm a serial entrepreneur, just like JP. Volunteering at church led to feeding the homeless, where the image of a catering truck popped into my head and Mobile Loaves & Fishes was born. Building relationships with men and women on the street led me to the conclusion that the greatest cause of homelessness is a profound catastrophic loss of family. What these people needed was a supportive community to keep them from falling through the cracks. That led me to the idea of building a kind of campground dedicated to the homeless. I acquired fifty-one acres of land just outside of Austin, built a lot of micro homes and Community First! Village was born. Our vision is to lift people out of the streets, allow them to heal from the ravages of living on the streets, then reconnect them back to themselves and their community, if not to their families. We can't fix everyone, but we can give people a helping hand and a chance to fix themselves. To live here you need to be a chronically homeless individual with a disability, who has lived in the streets of Central Texas for at least a year or up to a year over a four-year period.

We want to give everybody a hand up, not a hand out. There are about 450 people living in homes now at Community First! and we are working on building 1400 more. In addition to helping build homes, I funded their

Entrepreneur Hub where people can make art, ceramics, and jewelry. They also grow organic vegetables, fruit trees, and so much more. Residents can learn a skill and sell their products at the Community Market or online. In the first year and a half, formerly homeless people sold almost two-hundred thousand dollars worth of crafts and goods. Two of them also got a commission with a five-star hotel in Austin to do all their artwork. That's how good they are. Does entrepreneurship work? It sure does. People do amazing things with just a little bit of help.

Me and Eloise at Mobile Loaves & Fishes in Austin, TX

Photo credit: Constance Dykhuizen

From Alan Graham

I first met JP through a guy I hired to manage our farming operation. He met Constance Dykhuizen at a little church in East Austin. JP came out for a tour and loved our farming deal. His first gift was one-hundred-thousand dollars to help us enhance it. The people we were helping couldn't afford good organic vegetables and free range or heirloom anything. Now our Genesis Garden has a farmers market every Saturday. Everything we harvest is distributed to the men and women who live here.

I consider JP a friend. When he drives out to the Village, he's just one of us. He's comfortable around our people and they admire him. He's gotten involved with us and he's not afraid to share that with his friends and acquaintances and sometimes they help us too. We call it the halo effect. JP has a heart bigger than Dallas, Texas. He has an incredible ability to communicate well with people who've had a difficult and traumatic life. And he's sincere.

A few years ago, before Thanksgiving, Constance called to say that JP, Eloise, and other family members wanted to come out and serve Thanksgiving dinner here. Dinner was planned but the person had backed out. We were going to put together a Frito Pie buffet for people and invited them to come. Ten minutes later, Constance called back and said, "No way is John Paul DeJoria going to let people eat Frito Pie on Thanksgiving Day Y'all figure out where the turkey and dressing and everything else is coming from, but he's gonna write the check for the whole damn thing." And JP cut the turkey. That's who that man is!

Alan Graham is the real deal. Here's the crazy part—you'd expect him and his wife Tricia to live in a beautiful big house out in the country. Nope. They live in the middle of the village—in a mobile home that used to be his office. Tricia is the director of Neighbor Care and arranges all the activities. Alan is the CEO. His job is two-sided. He keeps up his relationships with politicians and the business people he knew when he was in real estate. They can be a big help when he needs it. But he also builds relationships with the people who live in the community.

Alan makes no bones about the fact that he's a Christian, but he doesn't push his beliefs on other people. Community First! Village was built on the foundations of the Gospel: to love God and to love our neighbors. Alan Graham lives what he preaches.

The first time we heard of Mobile Loaves and Fishes was when John Anthony was at Trinity Middle School. The kids would give out sandwiches that their mothers made for the homeless.

Before JP's Peace, Love & Happiness Family Foundation, I admit my giving was kind of disorganized. Thanks to Constance and her hard work, my donations have increased because I can see how it has given so many people a leg up. Giving to these organizations and getting to know leaders like Lisa and Alan has brought great joy to my life.

Chapter 16

Getting Water to Populations

It's amazing how many people don't have easy access to fresh water. It's not just in poor countries, but here in the United States too. Water makes all the difference and not just for growing. Lack of clean water means more disease, more death. In some places, I can make a big difference with a little bit of money. And I'm proud to say, I've met some incredible people doing it too.

Water for the Dine Nation

The first thing I ever did for water was with the Dine Nation. They're part of the Navajo Indians and live by the four corners of Arizona, New Mexico, Colorado, and Utah. Lisa Law, a photographer and pal who did a documentary that I funded about the Woodstock era, told me about them and I went there to visit. It was back in 1990.

Their history is complicated, but the bottom line was this. The federal government had divided the territory between the Hopis and Navajos, giving an area called Black Mesa to the Hopis who didn't even live there. Then they made a deal with the Hopi Tribal Council to put a lot of pressure on the Navajo Indians to relocate from their Big Mountain reservation at Black Mesa in Arizona. Why did they want them to leave? It turned out that the Black Mesa region had the largest coal deposit in the United States and the mining companies, especially the Peabody Coal Company, wanted to strip mine it.

Thousands of Dines left under pressure, but about 300 families had stayed on the reservation. It was mainly elderly ladies and a few men too. There were probably only one or two people that were over ten years old and younger than fifty. The problem was that no wells were available on their land. These ladies had to drive in a car for twenty to thirty minutes to get water and bring it back. I knew I could help. I drilled the first well for them so they had water right there on their land. But I wanted to do more. Lisa could have made a documentary about their situation, but they needed practical help.

The elders resisted the government's plans to make them leave. They tore down fences and blocked Peabody's bulldozers with their own bodies. They turned away the government officials who tried to persuade them to leave, sent emails to make the Navajo people more aware, and filed lawsuits accusing Peabody of unfair land use. But they needed to make money to survive. The Dine women were known for their weaving so I bought them a flock of Navajo-Churro sheep. Those are special long-haired sheep with more lanolin in their wool. They could shear the sheep and make their rugs and blankets from the wool.

A woman named Arlene Hamilton was working on the weaving project, and we wanted to make sure these women made a fair profit from their work. Their work could take as long as three months to make a rug, and we didn't want it going to trading posts where they'd get maybe forty dollars for it. Instead, we set up a retail division where we could sell their creations straight to the end customer or to the retailer and get anywhere from one-thousand to two-thousand dollars for each piece. The money people paid for these works of art now went right back into their hands. It changed their lives which made me feel great.

Meanwhile, Peabody Coal was in their backyard digging up their ancient burial grounds. Native Americans have a different attitude toward the land than the rest of us. They don't believe in owning land. To them, the earth is a sacred space and they need to be in balance with it. And there was another problem. Peabody delivered the coal with a slurry pipeline. It used a lot of water to send coal to its destination and dried up many of their springs. It also poisoned the water that the people needed for drinking and growing crops.

Arlene Hamilton worked with a Dine woman named Roberta Blackgoat. She lived on the reservation in a Navajo structure called a hogan. Roberta was one of the resisters. She was upset with what was happening to her home but didn't know what to do. I had an idea so I bought ten shares of Peabody stock and gave it to them. Hanson Industries in England had recently acquired forty-five percent of Peabody.

When Peabody Coal had their next board of directors meeting, I put Arlene Hamilton and Roberta Blackgoat on a plane and flew them to the board of directors meeting in England. Even though they had only ten shares, they were now official shareholders, so they signed up to talk. Roberta spoke broken English, but Arlene could talk for her. She spoke both English and Dine. Lord Hanson was there himself and the event planners thought there was going to be a problem, so they put security people around Roberta Blackgoat in case they had to remove her.

Roberta was smart. The first thing she said was, "Lord Hanson, first I want to thank you for giving me all this security. No one's going to hurt me." In other words, she made it a positive. Then she said, "Lord Hanson, you're not aware of this, I know, but Peabody's people are digging up old burial grounds." It was an unbelievable thing she did. She had him against a wall.

He said, "I'm going to take care of that immediately. I didn't know this was going on."

Making the Dine Indian Nation shareholders changed everything for them. And all it cost was ten shares. We stopped the coal mining. We stopped their Indian burial ground from going away.

The water access we gave them allowed them to grow their own vegetables. The Churro sheep kept multiplying and they can now make all the rugs and everything else they want. I'm so grateful to Lisa Law, who was there every single day I spent with the tribe, and for introducing me to the Dine Nation and these amazing women.

A federal judge ruled that Peabody's pipeline was guilty of violating the National Environmental Policy Act and the Surface Mining Control Act. The judge revoked Peabody's mining permit. Peabody appealed the decision and continued fighting for reestablishing mining access after this ruling.

Matthew McConaughey, Yeah Samake and Me;
Matthew is also active in helping Mali's development projects
Photo courtesy of author's personal collection

Digging Wells in Mali

I met Yeah Samake through a business friend in 2012. He was from Mali, secured a scholarship to attend Brigham Young University, graduated, and returned to Mali. When we met, Yeah explained that his country is one of poorest nations on earth. About two thirds of the country of Mali is in the Sahara Desert, so access to clean water is a big issue. A majority of villages don't have access to water and people sometimes have to walk miles to collect it for cooking and bathing even if it was often very contaminated. People would get sick when they drank it. How could I not do something to help these people?

From Yeah Samake

Since my first meeting with JP, we've made great strides in Mali's development. Eighty percent of my people live in rural areas which don't have access to basic resources like clean water. My foundation, Empower Mali, implements most of our projects in these areas. To help us meet the growing need for clean water in our villages, JP donated two-hundred-fifty thousand dollars to buy a drilling rig which we take from village to village to drill wells. Mali has a lot of underground water that's very clean, but sometimes very deep. Before we drill, we do a geological study to determine if the water can be reached and what way it will flow. We dig a well, sometimes as far as fifteen hundred feet deep. We install a solar pump and a five-thousand-litre water tank which stores the clean water, so it is accessible even on cloudy days. Additionally, we install water faucets throughout the village that allow the villagers to easily access this water. Most of the villagers have never seen a tap before. They think this water is magical. When the water first pumps out, the whole village rushes to wash their faces, hoping it will cure them. This project has saved lives and changed the landscape of many villages. Not only can our women grow gardens to improve nutrition and increase their income through other businesses because they have more time, but our girls remain in school because they don't have to spend many valuable hours fetching water at far away water spots.

Before JP's generosity, due to scarce water, villagers often had to choose between cooking water or bathing well, so cleanliness was not a priority in many villages. Now you can see the difference. As of 2025, we have seventy-two water systems in seventy-two different villages with many more in progress.

Building Schools

It wasn't just water they needed in Mali. Children had to travel three to five miles one way to get to schools because many villages did not have their own schools. Due to the dangers of the journey and the time involved, this meant many parents would keep their girls at home. The government didn't have the resources to build the schools they needed in these remote areas, so we started building schools for them. We worked out a great arrangement. We wanted it to be a partnership and asked the villages to help build the schools and provide some of the cost of labor. The government helps by providing paid teachers. That way everybody has a stake in the game.

From Yeah Samake

I lived in America for about twelve years, but America doesn't need me. The people of Mali do. I came from dire poverty and I'm now in the one percent of my people with master's degrees because of the education I have. I'm blessed to be where I am and now, I can impact a whole nation. I went back to my own community to give back to them. As a mayor, I helped build one of the largest hospitals in the region and the biggest solar panel field in my community. These were all things I couldn't do from America.

I have run for President of Mali twice and I plan to run again. Being a leader is all about service in my mind. I spend a lot of time in the villages, talking to people and explaining my vision. None of this could happen without JP. Our relationship is built on truth. I trust him and he trusts me. He would love to travel to Mali to see what we've done, but security issues are a problem. I love JP. He's humble, generous, drawn to serving, and wants to transform lives. He may be oceans away, but he's just as excited to serve the people of Mali as I am.

Adding happiness in Mali with water wells and schools

Photo courtesy of Constance Dykhuizen

Yeah tells me I'm a celebrity in Mali. He has my name plastered all over the country. JP's Peace, Love & Happiness Family Foundation is written on water tanks and schools. I love to see videos of Malian children dancing around, excited because they have water in their village for the first time or are able to go to a school close to them. Whole villages hold celebrations any time a school is opened or a well is dedicated.

Shark Tank and the Tree T-PEE

I was on Shark Tank in 2013 as a guest investor. I was only on once, but they replayed it hundreds of times. It was their biggest episode, and they won an Emmy for it. It was the most emotional show they have ever had in their history. A guy named Johnny Georges came on. He was a little farmer from Florida with something called the Tree T-PEE.

Johnny's story was interesting. His father, Rick Georges, invented a micro-sprinkler back in 1970 and it changed the whole irrigation industry. By bringing water to individual trees, it reduced the amount needed. After high school, Johnny started to work for his dad. Twenty years later, he'd learned a lot about irrigation. Back then, farmers used to bank trees whenever a frost was predicted. They'd pack dirt around the young trees to keep them warm and safe from the frost. Then they'd remove the dirt the next day. Johnny thought there had to be an easier way to protect young trees. So, his dad made a small cone to put around the base of the tree. But it still had to be removed after the frost.

Then Johnny came up with something better—the T-PEE. It was something that looked like a teepee. You put it around a tree and it gathered moisture at night so it didn't dissipate when the sun came out. You didn't need to water it that much nor did you need as much fertilizer. It kept it all within this Tree T-PEE. So, you use less water, less fertilizer, less electricity to pump the water into the micro-sprinkler. It was a win-win for farmers and the environment.

At first, Johnny had to face rejection from traditional farmers who wanted to hold on to their old practices. Little by little he chipped away at them, one farmer at a time, until he got his big break by appearing on Shark Tank in 2013. It happened to be the one time I was there. He offered the sharks a twenty percent stake in his business for a one-hundred-fifty-thousand dollar investment. Johnny was selling his product for about five dollars each. All the other sharks told him he had to charge more money. One of them even said, "You've got to charge at least twelve dollars, because we want to make a big profit from it. Johnny answered, "I can't charge them more. It's for farmers. Most don't have a lot of money. And they have a lot of trees so they won't be able to afford it." The other sharks all said, "I'm out." You could tell he was disappointed.

It was time for me to speak up. "Johnny," I said, "farmers are the cornerstone of America and a lot of them probably can't afford twelve dollars but maybe they can manage six dollars. I'm going to give you exactly what you're asking for. What you're doing is right and you deserve a chance to make it big. I'd like to be your partner, Johnny. I like everything you stand for."

The other sharks were surprised but one of them said, "Tell your dad he's a great man."

"He died twelve years ago," Johnny answered with tears in his eyes. After a long pause he said, "He made me who I am."

Eleven years later, Johnny's company, GSI Supply, is doing better. The cone-shaped tree T-PEE is used on trees that are one to five years old. Today's version contains one hundred percent of the water and fertilizer which is directed to the roots. In warm weather, the T-PEE is like a mini-greenhouse, keeping roots hydrated and increasing growth. It blocks the effects of wind and keeps water from being blown to areas where it isn't needed. During a frost, the warm water from the mist created by the mini-sprinkler inside rises up into the canopy of the tree, creating a "steam bath" effect.

Chapter 17
Passion Projects

Giving back has changed my life tremendously. Here's the best part: what I get back is so much more than I give. It's knowing I have a very powerful, positive effect on the world today. It's letting me see how strong a positive message can be. And it makes me feel even better and more worthy of being here. When you take yourself out of the equation, out of "what's in it for me," suppress your ego, and just give back to others, you'll be rewarded many, many times over. You don't even have to look for it. You'll feel it. It'll just come your way.

His Holiness, the 14th Dali Lama, and I met in 2000 and had a inspiring meeting . . . dialogue solves most of the world's problems

Photo courtesy of author's personal collection

Mozambique and the Run-Away Leg

Around 2001, I was in Mozambique, a nation on the southeast coast of Africa. Nelson Mandela, Sir Richard Branson, Brad Pitt and a few others besides myself were supporting a nonprofit organization called The Mineseeker Foundation. It was founded by a fellow who said he had discovered a method to detect buried landmines.

Mozambique had a serious problem with landmines left over from almost thirty years of war; first a war of independence and then a long civil war that ended in 1992. It was almost ten years later, and a lot of people were still losing arms, legs, and even their lives because of the landmines.

Nelson (Madiba) Mandela and Me in South Africa
Photo courtesy of author's personal collection

The foundation had two goals. One was to clear up the landmines and create Aid Free Zones so that the people could go back to developing land for agriculture and commercial purposes. The other goal was to provide prosthetics so people could become mobile and work again. At the time, we were waiting to get technology from the British government to fly a blimp over, find every landmine in the ground, and get rid of them. But they never delivered to us.

In the meantime, Nelson told me about his second wife, Graça Machel, who used to be the first lady of Mozambique. She'd been married to the first President of Mozambique who died in a plane crash years before. Nelson—we called him Madiba which comes from his Xhosa clan name—told me there were many people there without legs because they were blown up during the wars and after. Tribes would walk the opposing tribes of people across the field to clear the land mines. It was terrible!

I went into one of the main cities in Mozambique, where they were replacing limbs at a clinic. We worked with the Rotary Club of South Africa. What we did was measure people's limbs so they could be fitted for the right size. Prosthetics are different depending on the person. Did they lose their leg below the knee or above the knee? Are they a double amputee? It's not a case of "one leg fits all." Each prosthetic has to be customized to fit each person. Then you have to maintain the legs because of wear and tear.

This one lady, Maria, had lost both of her legs to a landmine. Fortunately, she didn't die, but the damage from the landmine came within an inch of her midsection. Maria was a hairdresser, but after the accident she had to hop on boxes to trim, cut, and braid people's hair. We said to her, "Okay, Maria, we're going to fix this for you." We measured while I was there. I made sure they had the money to give her two new legs. In the hospital, everyone's supposed to be in bed by dark, but at 10pm Maria was still walking all over the place. The staff tried to stop her. "Maria, you can't do that. You're still recovering."

Maria answered, "No, I've got legs. I can walk now," and refused to go to bed. She was so happy walking back and forth on her legs. Over time, Maria's legs were adjusted to fit her perfectly. She now has her own salon in Mozambique and can walk unencumbered with her prosthetic legs.

The people of Mozambique didn't always understand that the new legs were a permanent gift to them. The same day I was there, they fitted one guy with his finished leg. They put it on him but they still had to adjust it to fit him perfectly. All of a sudden, he was gone. Where did he go? We chased after him and found him on the street walking away. He was afraid we were going to take the leg from him and he wouldn't get it back! I told him, "No, no. We just want to make it right and adjust it perfectly." We brought him back, removed the leg, tweaked it, and returned it to him.

I'm happy to report that the country of Mozambique was cleared of all landmines in 2015.

Underprivileged Kids

I helped a guy name Bennie Davenport start a place in South Central LA called The Blazer Safe Haven Learning Center back in 1994. It's the same area where the Los Angeles riots happened in 1992. All the gangs at the time—the Crips, the Bloods, and all the others—agreed not to fight or do their hand signs within a three-block area of this site. We bought the place so all children in the area could get help after hours for grammar school, junior high, or high school. People tutored them with their homework and taught them how to use computers.

Muhammad Ali and his wife, Lonnie, joined my wife and me on one of our visits. The kids loved it. Twenty-five years later, The Blazers are still doing great work. They now have three core programs. They call them Academic Reinvestment, Sports Discipline, and Cultural Enrichment. It's basically a life mentorship program. If you go to their website, it'll tell you more about what they're doing but I can give you a quick recap.

The academic program doesn't just help children with school work. It teaches life skills and helps students become responsible members of society. It also teaches them how to make money, manage it, and invest it. We all know how important that is. The gardening and animal care programs teach good nutrition and how to care for animals. In the multimedia lab they learn about computers and other technologies that prepare them better for the work world.

And that's not all. The basketball sports program teaches important values like teamwork, respect, sportsmanship, determination, discipline, self-esteem and confidence. Then there's the cultural enrichment program that takes them out of a traditional classroom and exposes them to new career possibilities, cultures, and life experiences. Wow! You can see how being a part of The Blazers gives kids a boost up in the world and teaches them to be community leaders. I'm sure it gives a boost to all the volunteers, tutors and donors who make this nonprofit such a force for the community that surrounds it. I'm proud of my part in all of this.

Motorcycle Fundraisers

I love riding motorcycles. Remember I told you about my friend Lee Meyers, who gave me a place to stay the first time I had to live in my car? Lee and I would ride motorcycles on weekends. I didn't have one of my own, so I'd borrow from a friend. It was in the mid-sixties, and I got to be friends with many of his biker friends because Lee hung out with them.

Me and pal CB Sullivan (one of the first JPMS distributors) riding in a Sturgis Bike Week

Photo courtesy of author's personal collection

I'd drive up to Griffith Park where I could take my son for a ride on the merry-go-round for a quarter. The gangs used to hang out there, and they were so very nice to us. They understood my situation. I couldn't join them because I'd have to be with them all the time and I had to work. They were a rough group and got into a lot of fights, but they could be kind. They always treated me as if I was one of them, which was rare. They got it. They understood that I had a little child and had to work from early to late in order to support him.

A few years ago, I found out the San Fernando Valley Chapter of the Hells Angels was doing a Christmas fundraiser. It was to give toys to children whose parents were incarcerated. So, I went over to their clubhouse with my little hot rod full of toys for kids. It's kind of rare for a non-Hells Angels person to do, but I had a friend named Dennis who rode with them. We hung out that day, drank tequila, and had fun. Dennis and I have ridden motorcycles together a few times since then.

I've been doing motorcycle fundraisers for a long time now. It all started with a young guy I met around 1988. His name is Gary Spellman and he's one of my good pals. He was only twenty-two when we connected by chance in Newport, Rhode Island. He had no money and was working three jobs—one as a bouncer—to get through college. We hit it off from the first punch

———— ✳ ————

From Gary Spellman

I was working the door at a place called The Candy Store. I recognized John Paul because one of my jobs was in the beauty industry, selling shampoo for another brand. I let him cut the

line, then a young guy who was drunk grabbed me and said, "Who the hell is this guy?" I grabbed him back and we went to the ground. Then his friend, a rather large guy, jumped on my back. JP was just about to go into the club when he saw what was happening. He grabbed the big guy and went, "Let the man do his job." The big guy came up swinging and the next thing you know, it was like JP and I were in some swashbuckling movie, laying waste to the village in front of a crowd. It was a good thing my police friend showed up to handcuff them, because it looked like the whole crowd was going to jump in. After that, JP and I just connected. He sent me a first-class plane ticket to come visit him in Beverly Hills. And the rest is history.

For a while, Gary worked with a distributor in upstate New York who carried Paul Mitchell. I had to have a little meeting with him, because another distributor wasn't doing well with our products. We'd promised them a market and the best product, education, and service. We delivered but they weren't holding up their end of the bargain. In two years, Gary helped turn them around. After he met and married his wife Laurie, who was another Paul Mitchell distributor, he moved to Austin, Texas.

From Gary Spellman

Here's the thing about JP. If you strip away the cars, the houses, and the money, you still have a man of character and stature. He's also been generous with his time too. I once worked a show with him for JPMS. Angus was on stage cutting hair and there was a woman in the corner crying her eyes out. She said, "I missed my flight and it's my daughter's recital. I'm never going to make it in time to see my daughter's performance."

This woman lived in Houston and had never bought a Paul Mitchell product. I knew because I was the distributor for Houston. John Paul asked what was going on and I explained.

Then he walked up to her and said, "Tell you what. You come back here in a half hour with your luggage. I'll be right here and we'll get you home."

She asked, "How are you gonna do it?"

He said, "I have a jet."

We were supposed to fly from New York to Austin, but he had the plane touch down in Houston first. He also had a car waiting for her.

I don't celebrate birthdays because I think every day is my birthday. One day, Gary and I sat down and he suggested, "Let's do a charity motorcycle ride on your birthday. Your gift will be anything the riders donate to your charity, and JP, we can underwrite the entire event ourselves."

We called it the Peace, Love & Happiness Motorcycle Ride, and we have held it every year since then on or around my birthday. We raised seventy-five-thousand dollars in one day on one ride and gave the proceeds to the Austin Children's Shelter and Club 100, a Central Texas charity for first responders in need. This ride continues to raise money for paramedics, firefighters, law enforcement officers, and abused and neglected children. We have done other rides all around the country to raise money for disabled adults to find jobs, for veterans, and for special equipment for disabled people to live their lives to the fullest. It feels great to do good while doing something you love.

From Gary Spellman

We do these motorcycle fundraisers all over the country. And you never know who'll pop in to ride with us: Keanu Reeves, Peter Fonda, Jesse James, former Texas Gov. Rick Perry, Robin Leach, and many others. JP's legacy isn't his money or his companies. He isn't just a billionaire who gives back. To me, his legacy will always be his heart. And it didn't take a crisis in his life to make him that way. John Paul was just born with a gracious, giving heart.

I've got to tell you that JP also has a wicked sense of humor. Recently we did a motorcycle run for a charity during Daytona Bike Week. We were taking a table of ten out for dinner. Now JP always likes to pay, but I don't think it's fair so I made everyone rotate paying the bill. This time the bill was going to the son of one of our top customers. We were at a fancy steak house, and I know the bill was going to be high, at least twenty-five-hundred dollars. But JP didn't want to do that to this young man and he paid the bill in advance. The waiter brought the bill back for JP to sign. JP opened the bill and said, "Glad I'm not buying!" and handed it over to the young man. It only took a few seconds for him to catch on, and it's a perfect example of JP's generosity and mischievous humor.

Chapter 18

Barbuda, Costa Rica, Scotland, & Mexico

Barbuda is a small island in the Caribbean by Antigua. Together they are an independent country with a few smaller islands and a part of the British Commonwealth. I was looking to get into real estate and Charlie, a friend of mine, encouraged me to come see it. This was 2016. Barbuda is only a three-and-a-half-hour flight from Austin. But getting there was a little more complicated then. You needed to fly to Antigua first and either take a boat for two hours or a helicopter or a small plane to get there. I flew in by helicopter the first time and walked on the most beautiful beaches I'd ever seen in my life. Nine miles of beautiful beaches. When you took off your shoes, my God, the sand felt like powdered sugar.

But I could see Barbuda had problems at that time. Parts of the island were destroyed. The people had been doing what's called sand mining there. Much of the population was unemployed and subsidized. People didn't have work, so they were taking sand from their own sand dunes and selling it to other islands. It was crazy. They were wiping out their own environment. Historically, the island had a great sea turtle population but with no sand the turtles weren't coming back like they used to. Plus, a lot of people were poaching them. Then I saw that the reef was destroyed, mainly because of global warming. Most of the coral was gone and that meant a lot of fish had disappeared as well.

It was sad to see all this destruction, but I liked everyone I met on Barbuda. They were both welcoming and proud of their heritage. It was such a cool place. It was ideal. It was beautiful. Although I saw the possibilities of what it could be as a premier resort development, I wasn't just thinking about how it could be a prosperous business venture. It was as much about how I could really do something to help the people and the environment—how I could actually help change the whole island for the better—change it for the inhabitants, the ecosystem, and the people who were going to buy and build their dream homes in the resort we hoped to develop on Barbuda.

Creating a Plan

My friend Charlie introduced me to JB, who had identified an opportunity and done some of the early planning for a residential resort project on Barbuda. I put up the money and we engaged Discovery Land Company, founded by Michael Meldman, to develop and manage the project for us. I thought that Discovery was an excellent choice because they had a history of building high-end resort communities with every amenity you could ever imagine while keeping the environment in mind. My thinking was this: If I do a project here, it has to create opportunities and support the community. If it doesn't change anything on this island, it's not worth my doing it. While I'm alive I want to do things that benefit the planet. Then I feel cool. If it's just for monetary reasons, you don't get that same feeling and it's just not right. I met with Prime Minister Gaston Brown and told him what I wanted to do to change Barbuda for the better.

The prime minister said "JP, you represent us well, so how about being our ambassador at large for Antigua and Barbuda." I was honored to accept this position and now I have a diplomatic passport, which is pretty cool. And I can promote the islands of Antigua and Barbuda as a destination.

JB and I, together with Discovery Land Company, set out to develop a first-class residence club and resort called the "Barbuda Ocean Club." But we needed an environmental plan from the beginning. We brought in Dr. Deborah Brosnan, an expert marine biologist who is an authority on climate and ecology and she did an entire ecological scope of the island. The moment we met, I knew we were on the same page.

———— ✳ ————

From Dr. Deborah Brosnan

I met JP in early 2017. From the beginning I knew he was the kind of person I wanted to be involved with. He was the real deal. I love when you take the knowledge that science provides and start to apply it in the real world. With JP, I had to figure out how the ecosystem worked and how we could restore it when it's damaged. I also love working with local people because their way of life is most affected when nature gets into trouble. I love putting ecosystems and people together. With JP, I had to solve a third problem. How do you get a return on an investment for individuals or companies, because without their financial investment, stuff often doesn't get done. What struck me was what I now call the "JP guidelines." Do no environmental harm, provide economic benefit to the community, and use the best science available." Those are the guidelines that have driven everything we've done. We used the best science, engaged and trained local people in the work we do, and created an economic value as well as value for the ecosystem.

Hurricane Irma

Then on September 6, 2017, Category 5 Hurricane Irma hit Barbuda. It was a catastrophe. Everyone needed to be evacuated. Captain Paul Watson, an environmental activist who I've supported, had one of his ships down there. I paid for the fuel and everything else to help take people off Barbuda and put them in Antigua where they would be safe. The storm's eye passed right over Barbuda, causing walls of wind, storm surges, and flooding. Since many dunes were down to sea level, the storm surge from the hurricane just ran over the land. It destroyed farms and covered everything in saltwater. A lot of the vegetation died because of that. The situation in Barbuda went from bad to worse and I knew we had to do something. We had to bring the ecosystem back.

Rebuilding Barbuda's Ecology

First, we started to bring the sand dunes back. How did we do it? We got some of the sand out of the ocean. We were also building a golf course, so we started to dig. This is how you get commerce and ecology to work together. The rest of the sand came from the areas we had to dig out to create the lakes on the golf course that were part of the development design. We just dug and used that sand to bring the dunes back. When Deborah came on, we dug some more and created wetlands. The digging made beautiful lakes in the golf course and brought back the habitat with a magnificent watershed. I'm proud to say we now have a Fazio-designed coastal golf course with wetlands. The rebuilt sand dunes also gave the sea turtles a place to nest. We increased the turtle population in one year. Now people can watch the turtles breed and the little ones come out of their eggs. Then we went to work on the sea turtles themselves.

———— ✳ ————

From Deborah Brosnan

By restoring the dunes and adding native vegetation there, we were providing a habitat for sea turtles to nest. Still, many of the sea turtles were being poached because nobody was monitoring them. We found a local guy who had started monitoring sea turtles as a kid. One night his father had dragged him down to the beach and showed him a leatherback turtle that was nesting. He said it changed his life. He'd go out with pen and paper and he would draw pictures of the turtles and the markings on them. We got this guy to teach some of the local community that were interested in sea turtle monitoring. We hired these people to monitor the sea  *turtles and taught them more sophisticated ways over the years. The program is in its fourth year now and we have about ten monitors. They actually had a regional symposium last year and people from ten island nations came to Barbuda to participate. And it was all because of JP. No one told him to do it. Now a whole program exists when there was nothing.*

———— ✳ ————

Dr. Deborah Brosnan and Me in Barbuda
Photo courtesy of Dr. Brosnan

Then we said, "Let's do something about the reefs." We wanted to see if we could grow coral in the ocean. Deborah was responsible for the plan we called the Ocean Shot Project. We learned how to grow coral. How? We found various species that had survived global warming on the other side of the island and brought them over. And we were very successful. Then we started to make artificial reefs in Florida that were put on barges and brought over. They were specially designed so the fish would stay.

We planted the artificial reefs in the ground on one side. In one week, fish and squid started investigating. Sea urchins and other marine life not only stayed, they multiplied. We watched different creatures attaching over time. It was the most amazing thing. All the coral we had put in there, a total of six different species, were thriving. Nemo fish showed up. It worked! Within six months, the artificial reef was almost completely covered.

From Deborah Brosnan

Restoring the reefs was probably our biggest innovation. What happens when a reef dies is it starts to collapse because there's no living coral. As coral grows it secretes its own calcium carbonate. Without the coral there's nothing to grow the reef. That's what was happening in parts of Barbuda. Also, because of sea level rise, we were seeing erosion at the rate of ninety feet in less than eighteen months. It's a huge issue.

When JP and I started talking about what to do, I had an idea. If you look at what a reef structure does, it breaks the waves, keeps sand on the beach, and provides habitats for fish, invertebrates, and coral. If we could figure out the shape of a reef that does that and then build it and put it in place, in effect we'd be doing what Mother Nature does instead of building a breakwater.

So that's what we did. We literally designed a shape that looks like a coral reef with little holes and spaces for different species to live. We made our reefs from pH-neutral concrete. Certain species like to live in the penthouse and feed on plankton. Others like to live in the subways. So, we provided all the layers for them.

After the first year we put our homemade reefs out, we found thirty-six species of fish living there and a lot of invertebrates. The sea urchins, who are very fickle but very important for the reef, have all stayed. That tells us they recognize our reef as a habitat. We plan to build a reef on a bigger scale to cover a larger area of Barbuda. We'd like to get them made in Barbuda too. JP is building an innovation lab on Barbuda so we can do more of this kind of work. To be honest, there's not much of an economy there and this would provide a place for people to work and learn and have opportunities they wouldn't have otherwise.

Building an Economy for Barbuda

Our work isn't done yet. There is more we can do, not just for the people of Barbuda, but also the entire island habitat. We've created and restored two miles of sand dunes to date and contributed more than half a million dollars to community programs. We've brought back the turtle population.

The population of Barbuda was about 1,600 when I first went there. Everybody had to leave because of the hurricane, but only a fraction came back. And most needed jobs. Our aim is to give a job to anyone who wants one.

We also help support the local population in a lot of other ways. We operate two small stores on the island to provide affordable essentials. I was worried about what people were eating and we built all-organic gardens. Now the people who live there have better access to fresh food. And we're teaching the islanders how to grow food in our gardens. We also operate two small medical facilities for staff, contractors, and our club members. We even brought in an ambulance and a fire truck. We provide free wi-fi and internet access to a local primary school through one of my companies, ROKiT Cities.

We've created a program to teach people how to be entrepreneurs. We offer interest-free loans to our staff to assist with housing and furniture and for business ventures supported by an approved business plan. Over forty percent of our staff have taken out loans from us. We hired a very smart man named Abishur Thomas. He didn't have work at the time and had no way to support his wife and two children. We saw his potential. We not only helped put him in business, but now, two years later, he has his own company with close to a dozen people working for him. We are his biggest customer. That's the kind of success story that makes me smile.

People are starting to come back to the island who left as teenagers or in their early 20s because there was no money there, nothing to do, no jobs. And they're coming home again, in many cases, to work for us. We even attract people from neighboring islands to come to Barbuda for opportunities. I'm hopeful that we can employ as many as a thousand people full-time at the Barbuda Ocean Club.

The Barbuda Ocean Club

We learned a lot from Hurricane Irma when it came to designing the houses in the Barbuda Ocean Club project. How big was the surge? It was about three feet. So, we ensured that all future builds were at least twelve feet above sea level. The center of the hurricane went through the island. It was a total wipe out. We asked, what if there was ever a Category 6? That's what we use as a "what-if" for how the houses at the project are built.

We made the decision to elevate everything by twelve feet but planned it in a way that no one will ever see it. You see, the sand dunes cover all that support structure under the houses. The sand comes right up to the base of the house structures, and the steel and concrete below are buried out of sight. We put poles in the ground that are reinforced with steel and concrete. We drilled into the hard rock below and set the pillars in there. The idea is for the sand dunes to block the water when the surge comes in. We want to be prepared in case the worst hurricane imaginable comes through. We even built a 200-foot tower after Hurricane Irma, so residents would have better communication.

Scott Mitchell is the architect on my house there. I asked him, "Scott, if you think this is built so well, does that mean you'd be willing to stay here with me when the next big hurricane comes through?"

His answer was, "JP, I will be there and that is a promise."

We also helped plan, manage, and fund the work on a 7,000-foot runway so big jets can land there. That's important because a high percentage of the typical Discovery Land Company buyers and club members own private jets.

The project did cost a lot more money than we thought. Of course, we didn't plan on Hurricane Irma, but we were able to use the event to gather information and get an education. In addition to the work to restore core infrastructure we had to deal with shortages because everything had to be brought in from off the island. All of that really added to the costs of the project. We've had a couple of critics who say, "Look, they are destroying the island with all of their excavating and building."

Deborah and I were keynote speakers at the World Ocean Summit in Lisbon, Portugal. We were asked to explain how we did this project. How did we incorporate big business and ecology to not only make the land better, but also make it beautiful for the people living there, for the investors in the homes being built, and for the wildlife? We took commerce and ecology and mixed the two together. Now both local islanders and people buying multi-million-dollar houses can go down to the beaches with their children and grandchildren and watch the sea turtles being hatched. They can also walk to the water's edge to see our beautiful reefs teeming with life again.

From Deborah Brosnan

Most wealthy people wouldn't have gone along with my suggestions about combining science with nature. They would probably say, "Oh, that's such a hard-engineering approach. But JP believed in it. He believed in what I was doing. And he believed in me. Together, we've been able to do this truly remarkable work in Barbuda. And people are beginning to take notice which is great. I believe that Barbuda is going to become the gold standard for what other islands and countries can do in the Caribbean.

The work never would have happened without JP's financial support. It's not just about money. Most people don't interact with the local people but JP does. Most of the islanders are shy around him at first. I saw him once go up to a group of them and say, "You're the sea turtle team." Within about thirty seconds they went from being afraid to talk to him to having a lovely conversation with him. I watched as their hearts opened up. And all he does is just go up to them and start talking. It's like they know somebody sees them for who they are.

The Barbuda Ocean Club employs a huge number of local people. They work on the construction of the buildings and the golf course. The company also gives them interest-free business loans, and a chance to become micro-entrepreneurs. These are people who depended to a large extent for many years on social welfare. And now just about anyone who wants a job, gets one.

Resort Real Estate—Costa Rica

I became interested in land and development projects right around the time we invested in Barbuda, and I now have three other large-scale, residential resort properties I'm developing with Discovery Land Company. With each investment, besides financial success, keeping ecological balance is priority number one. I'm making sure the people we hire respect the environment and design projects that are beautiful. I work with them to make sure they follow through. Priority number two is putting local people to work.

I bought two thousand acres (with my friend from the home office, Kevin) and two beaches in Costa Rica. This is home to the Zapotal Golf & Beach Club. We're putting local people to work there while taking care of the ecology of the area. I think it will be one of the finest destinations, private residences and resorts in all of Central and South America.

I'm also working closer to home with Discovery Land Company on a project near Austin, Texas called the Driftwood Golf & Ranch Club.

Historic Real Estate—Scotland

I am really excited about my project in the Highlands of Scotland, known as the Taymouth Castle Golf and Sports Club, another Discovery Land Company development. Let me tell you where it started. We went on a classic car tour with twenty friends to drive and see Scotland. Lunch was catered in a partially restored, very big castle. The original castle on the site was completed in 1550, but it was later demolished. Taymouth Castle was built in the 1800s, with completion just in time for a visit by Queen Victoria and Prince Albert in 1842 as guests of the second Marquess of Breadalbane.

Taymouth Castle Golf and Sport Club

With the advice of my friend Henry, a British gentleman with a great sense of humor, I put up the money to buy the castle and over the last many years, working through Discovery Land Company, I fully restored it. Today it is one of the two finest, privately-owned castles in all of Scotland. It offers many amenities including the best salmon and wild trout fishing, horseback riding, a first-class health center, and a golf course that they tell me was designed by the Godfather of Golf.

Taymouth Castle Golf and Sport Club

The renovation was completed with the help of the historical society. My friend Kevin and I bought the land adjacent to the castle and its grounds. Today, there are almost eight thousand acres of land available for the guests to enjoy.

Fun Real Estate—Mexico

Walter Staudinger and I have been good friends for over forty years. Together, we helped create a fun project in the little picturesque Mexican town of Sayulita. We built a unique, high-quality hotel with about fifty rooms offered at a very realistic price. There is entertainment every night in the streets and even surfers can afford to stay there! If you have experience with an honest, smart and fun friend like Walter . . . your time brings you more joy and more confidence in anything you do. Walter and I have other things going on, too.

Thoughts on Real Estate

With the exception of Taymouth Castle, which is a project focused on historic preservation and beautification of the castle and the surrounding property, these developments are designed for the best of everything. Still, I feel good about how we're doing these projects. Paying attention to the ecology of the area and bringing back land that's been damaged benefits everyone. Hiring local people gives them a leg up and keeps them happy and secure. Including investors and buyers in the process gives them a sense of ownership in the entire community. That's important to me.

The first question I always ask myself when I make any real estate decision is, "Would I want to live here? Is this a place I'd enjoy staying for an extended period of time with my family?"

My answer on all of my projects is "Absolutely!"

Now everyone can see what I dreamed about during those early days. Taking care of the environment and helping the people who've always lived there is good business. It makes me feel happy too.

Chapter 19

North Korea

People often ask me, "Why do you think you've been asked to help with issues in foreign countries?" and "Why would any of these people even listen to you?" Heck, if you'd asked me before if I saw myself as someone who could influence international leaders, I would have said, "Absolutely not!"

But I've found that a lot of people—even those in high levels of power who are feared—seem to pay attention to people who tell it like it is. I'm a very down-to-earth and friendly person. People know that about me. Even Muammar Gaddafi said that I was the only one who did what I did without asking for anything in return. Maybe it's because of the energy he felt from me . . . and he liked me. I guess it helps that I've been successful in a lot of things I've done. Going into North Korea happened totally by accident. When Kim Jong-Il saw that show about me on *Pinnacle,* he said, "Get this guy in here."

Here's how I ended up in North Korea. My wife and I were at the Imperial Hotel in Vienna, Austria. The year was 1996. Kim Il-Sung had died the year before and his son, Kim Jong-Il had succeeded him as leader of North Korea. Eloise and I were watching a *CNN* program called *Pinnacle* which was hosted by Beverly Schuch and was about my life. It took them months to make this special which we shot in the United

215

States. It was shown worldwide so we were able to watch it in Vienna.

Within twenty-four hours, we got a phone call. The United States embassy in Beijing had received a call from Pyongyang, North Korea's capital. They wanted to contact me. The embassy, I think, called my offices who got in touch with me and said, "You're not going to believe this!"

They told me Kim Jong-Il had seen me on television and said, "That's the guy who wrote the letter." And that's how we got invited over there.

Now I have to go back a bit and tell you about the letter. George Lee was our Paul Mitchell distributor in South Korea. He'd gone to a nice restaurant in Beijing (Peking at the time) and seen some Koreans at a table nearby. He went over to drink with them. George discovered that they were North Korean intelligence people. They told him they wanted to get an American to help them industrialize.

Of course, George knew me and had seen the presentations I gave. He said, "I've got just the guy for you, John Paul DeJoria. He was homeless and became a millionaire with the Paul Mitchell business. He loves to help train people in trades, colleges, and any kind of business."

They said, "Great! Invite him to meet us by John Paul DeJoria sending a letter."

George told me about this, and I said I didn't know but I'd see if there was a way I could do it legally. So, I contacted the U.S. government. They said I could go but I couldn't spend more than one-hundred dollars there. They also said I could write them whatever I wanted, but I wouldn't be allowed to engage in business with them until the United States lowered the trade barrier. They also told me that the North Koreans had already contacted other industrialists and there was no way in hell they'd choose me. I had a beard, wore my hair in a ponytail, and was in the hair-care and spirits business. No way! I sent a letter to Kim Jong-Il anyway and forgot about it.

So that phone call no more than twenty-four hours after he watched the program about me on *Pinnacle* was unreal. Kim Jong-Il was inviting me over. At the time, I was a part of Greenpeace with Mikhail Gorbachev, who gave me a letter introducing me as a great guy. I also got a letter from Dr. Noel Brown who was Director of the United Nations Environment Program. Kim Jong-Il had invited me and one other person to come to his country as his guest. Dr. Brown's letter introduced me as being associated with the United Nations.

Eloise thought it would be an amazing experience for my daughter, Alexis, so I should take her as the other guest. She was about eighteen at the time. Can you imagine that kind of experience as a teenager? The two of us went over together. We flew into Beijing, then took Air Koryo, their national airline, over to North Korea.

On the plane with us was a North Korean Ambassador who attended the Geneva talks; we'd seen him on television a month earlier. He was trying to get the U.S. and China to agree to meet with North Korea in three-way talks about South Korea. We wanted four-way talks. North Korea refused. They said South Korea was a puppet of the United States.

Only a few other people were seated in the front of the plane; my distributor, George Lee (who spoke perfect Korean), Alexis and me. We saw two Mercedes limos pull up, followed by two buses, with journalists and cameras. Some men opened the first limousine door for the number one guy and bowed to him. He got out of the car and walked up the steps. He walked right past us and greeted their ambassador in Korean, then led him to the steps. The number one guy then turned around and came directly back to us. He said, "John Paul DeJoria and Alexis DeJoria, welcome to the People's Republic of Korea."

His name was Kim In-chol. We got off the plane and he said, "John Paul, George Lee and your daughter will ride in the second limousine and just you and me in this limousine."

I said, "No, I'm not going to leave my daughter out of my sight."

"JP," he said, "everyone knows you're here. If anything goes wrong, it will destroy any diplomacy we have. You are a guest of Kim Jong-Il and you and your daughter will stay in the Palace."

We complied with the request and then he put us up at the Palace. It was VIP treatment for us. Without exaggerating, my bedroom was about forty feet square. I was in the same room Mao Tse-tung stayed at when he was visiting. My office was also about forty feet square. Unbelievable.

I showed Kim In-chol the letters I had from Gorbachev and the United Nations. He said it was okay to show the letter from the U.N. but not the one from Gorbachev. When I asked why, he said that Gorbachev's Perestroika movement showed that communism didn't work and needed to be restructured. "So don't show that letter to anyone." I didn't.

They drove us all over the country in Mercedes cars and a train ride. One place they took us was their school of music. It was in a beautiful, communist-looking, cement building. We went inside and all the kids were dressed like little Korean dolls in old, traditional clothes. Their music performance was like an orchestra, well-done and beautiful. Then we went up to the second or third floor. The guy who handled us there spoke perfect English even though he'd never left North Korea. He said, "We have here the greatest music library in the world. North Korea has the greatest of everything. Pick any song you want. We'll play it."

Alexis said, "Any Led Zeppelin song."

He went, "Come on, there's no such thing."

I said, "Alexis, they may not be aware of certain things, so let's go easy on these people."

Then she said, "How about Elton John?"

He answered, "You're messing with us. He must be a little artist. You know we only know the big ones, not the little ones that you may know but nobody else knows."

"Okay, Michael Jackson." He didn't have a clue.

I said to Alexis, "We're going to load them up now," and I suggested the Beatles.

"Ah, you're joking with us. Those are bugs. We know what a beetle is. Give us one of your real big artists."

We came back with, "Elvis Presley."

Didn't have a clue. That's how closed that society is in North Korea.

In the end, he said, "We're going to play for you your most popular song of them all."

I thought this should be interesting. And what comes on?

Chim chiminey, Chim chiminey, Chim, chim, cher-ee.

Of course, it's a famous song from *Mary Poppins*. We didn't say a word because we were advised things like this would happen. We just said, "Thank you" in Korean.

On our second day there, Kim In-chol took me to a meeting with a gentleman who was in charge of the North Korean economy, along with many other ambassadors, advisors, and those who examined North Korea's economy. My daughter didn't come to this one. He sat me next to a lady who was the interpreter. On the other side of me was their head of industry. This guy started to tell me about everything bad the United States had done.

"You killed our people," he said. "The United States Navy went into our country during the Korean War and were blowing our people up. We know you were in the United States Navy, and you were killing our people."

I got this funny feeling. Maybe it was just me being me, but I started laughing. The place went silent. This guy looked at me as if he was going to kill me. I looked at him and said to the interpreter, "Would you please tell the honorable (whatever his name was) that it would have been impossible. I was only seven or eight years old at the time. I couldn't have killed anybody. And, by the way, when I was in the Navy I was in communications and a dental technician. I would never have killed anyone."

After that, Kim In-chol came up to me and said, "John Paul, you'll be fine. I'm going to meet with Kim Jong-Il right now. You have all your security with you, even though you don't need it, and your daughter will see you back at the Palace for lunch."

That was when I talked to them about ecology and helping to develop their country. My goal on behalf of the United Nations was simple. I said, "When you do reunify, as either a unified country or a federation of the North and South (we were hopeful back then), would you agree to take out all the landmines from that two-mile-deep demilitarized zone that goes across the whole peninsula and make it into a park for all of Korea to enjoy?" They seemed to think it was a great idea.

I also brought up the four-way talks that the man from Geneva had mentioned. The proposed peace talks to be attended by North Korea, South Korea, China, and the United States were an effort to resolve tensions at the North and South Korean borders. I promised them if they went to the four-way talks, nice things would happen. "Don't be afraid," I said.

After I returned home to the United States, the North Koreans invited Eloise and me to their diplomatic mission in New York City. It was a big deal because they never let anyone in there. We met their key guy at the mission and his assistant and brought them to our house in Malibu. They spent a couple of nights with us and we got really chummy. It was shortly after their visit, by the way, that North Korea agreed to the four-way talks. My visit may have had an impact. That trip was a really cool experience.

One more thing happened because of my trip to North Korea.

While I was there, I realized the people were going through a famine. Hundreds of thousands of people in North Korea were dying of hunger. This was 1996. I worked with the State Department and a group from the University of Michigan to buy ten thousand pounds of vegetable seeds to ship over there. I was afraid if I sent money it would disappear. Several months later, I turned it over to the State Department. I said, "Here's what I've done. Call me if you need me." The State Department may have begun sending food to North Korea. It's been estimated that as many as three million people may have died from that famine.

I'm optimistic that things will change some day in North Korea. The people there deserve it. I don't know if the economy ever fully recovered from the famine. It still depends on food aid from the international community. The people of the country are great, but they don't know what's going on in the outside world. It's such a closed off country you can't get one signal in.

A note to the story: When we arrived in Peking (now Beijing) to catch a plane, we stayed overnight and met with Mike Chinoy, who was the CNN correspondent for all of Asia. I promised him when I left, I would do an interview. After leaving North Korea, we flew back to Peking, and I met with him. He did a four or five-minute special on my visit to North Korea and it was all about turning the demilitarized zone into an ecology zone. That report went world-wide.

I never took credit for my role in all this. I didn't even want a press conference. Let the government handle it, I thought. There's still hope for the demilitarized zone to become a part of peace in North Korea. I haven't given up on them and I'm still willing to help.

Chapter 20

Shell Oil in Africa

About a year after the North Korean trip, in 1997, I was still working with Dr. Noel Brown who was with the United Nations. He knew all about my visit to North Korea because he was part of it. I was going to Europe, and we were talking all the time. This one time I was going to be in London, he said, "Is there any way in the world you could help us out with a project? You seem to get along with people, and we have a real problem we're trying to solve. We're against the wall now."

Then he told me about the Ogoni people, a tribe of about five hundred thousand who had lived in the oil-rich area of Nigeria for five hundred years. In the 1950s, the Shell Oil Company discovered oil in the Niger Delta where the Ogoni lived. For decades, their oil had leaked into the land, destroying fields, making water undrinkable, and harming the local population.

The Nigerian government, I was told, was a military dictatorship. Any money from Shell Oil went to the government and none to the Ogoni people, who were a different tribe. I was told by Dr. Noel Brown of the United Nations that the Ogoni people were killing Shell Oil personnel in the field because they were ruining their land and they were receiving nothing in return.

Noel said, "JP, here's what we need. We need for the head of Shell Oil or some big people there to talk directly with the Ogoni people and clean up the mess they made with all their oil and make sure they get something for pillaging their land. We just need that meeting to happen; what can you do?" He said that if I could do something it would be great. If not, I was already there, so why not give it a try?

I was in London, England, and I found out that Shell's public relations office was in London too. So, I called them and because of my name and influence, I got to the head of their public relations who talked to me. I thought he was a nice fellow at the time.

I said, "You may not know me, but your wife may because of Paul Mitchell hair care products. I'm going on *BBC* tomorrow about what we're doing at Hyde Park on behalf of hairdressers. But I'm here for another reason." Then I told him about the situation with the Ogoni and the United Nations' request.

He explained, "I know all about the situation. Please understand this. We only deal with the government in Nigeria. We don't deal with individual tribes. I'll carry your message on, sir. And thank you for being interested."

"Sir," I said, "Dr. Noel Brown of the United Nations is the one who suggested I try to help here. All I want to do is arrange for the head of Shell Oil and the head of the Ogoni people to talk to one another. They, in return, will stop killing."

He continued to say that they only deal with the government.

I was getting impatient. "Okay. Here's what I'm going to do. I'm going on *BBC* tomorrow, and they're going to ask why I'm here. I'm going to tell them about Hyde Park and Paul

Mitchell. Then I'm going to say, 'But there's another reason I'm here—in conjunction with the United Nations, I'm trying to get the Shell Oil people to talk to the Ogoni people of Nigeria, because Shell is devastating their land and not giving them any money as compensation. But Shell won't talk to them. They say they'll only talk to the people who are running the country, the ones who are getting their money and not the Ogoni people.'"

He said, "Whoa! What?"

I repeated myself.

Then he said, "Don't do anything, don't say anything. Please give me a couple of hours with this one. John Paul, you're very sincere, let me see what I can do." Within a matter of a few hours, he called back and said, "Shell Oil had planned to do that anyway."

He was embarrassed and I knew he wasn't telling the truth. Anyway, I told him how to get in touch with Dr. Noel Brown and I immediately called Brown myself. He congratulated me. He talked directly to the top people at Shell who agreed to talk to the Ogoni people.

Chapter 21
Gaddafi

What happened in North Korea may have helped when I went to see Colonel Gaddafi, probably because I never took any credit and was very low key about it. I think Gaddafi was perhaps buying bio-weapons or cruise missiles from North Korea at the time, and they may have told him, "JP came in, did nothing but good stuff, and we never heard anything from him afterwards. He was just a good guy. Period."

It all started when an associate and good friend of mine at the time, Jerry, asked for a favor. He said, "JP, I know what you did in North Korea and for the Ogoni people. We have a situation, and I wonder if you'd like to help us out with it?" He explained to me he had met with Omar Muntasir a year earlier, who was Colonel Gaddafi's chief of staff, and Gaddafi.

Two of Colonel Gaddafi's people were responsible for the bomb that exploded on Pan Am Flight 103 in 1988. It was the plane that went down over Lockerbie, Scotland and was considered the deadliest terrorist attack in the United Kingdom. Two hundred seventy people died, including all the passengers, crew members, and eleven people on the ground. After a three-year investigation, the United States FBI and the Scottish Constabulary issued arrest warrants for two Libyan nationals in 1991. It was now around the year 2000 and the United Nations had been negotiating with Gaddafi to release the men for trial. Gaddafi wanted the U.N. to lift its sanctions on Libya. It was one of the requirements.

My friend explained, "JP, we need someone to convince Gaddafi that what we're saying in the agreement is real. He does not trust it. He has done every single thing the United States of America has asked him to do. Every single thing except for giving up the two suspected terrorists of Pan Am Flight 103. He has already denounced terrorism and given up all his terrorism training camps, his biological weapons and his missiles. The one thing he hasn't done is turn over those two suspects."

After I agreed, I was then given background information on the subject, and I arranged a flight into Tunisia. Because of our trade embargo, I couldn't fly directly into Libya. So, I flew on my own dollar in a little jet from England to Tunisia. Everything was arranged in advance for me by my contact. After I arrived in Tunisia, I was picked up in a beautiful Mercedes limousine by two Libyan agents. They drove me for about eight hours to Tripoli. It was the only legal way for me to get in.

They put me up in a hotel in Tripoli along with Jerry. We were there for a couple of days to meet Gaddafi but never saw him. Then they moved us to Sirte where we checked into another hotel. At eleven o'clock that night there was a knock on my door. I opened it and a gentleman stood there and said, "Omar Muntasir sent me to pick you guys up." He was Gaddafi's chief of staff.

The man continued, "I'm going to knock on your friend's door and wake him up. Get dressed right away!"

Within ten minutes we were dressed and out the door with him. Gaddafi's men drove us over maybe an hour into the desert. When we got out of the car, we were frisked from head to toe. Then they put us in a military Jeep and drove us through the desert with all the lights off.

We drove for at least another half hour. This guy knew every sand dune and how to get there. Finally, we saw in the distance five tents, very dimly lit. We had been told before that Gaddafi moves every single night. He never stays in the same place twice because he's afraid someone will kill him or blow him up.

We approached the first dimly lit tent. Our escorts stopped, looked at me and the other gentleman, and said, "Stand right here." Right here was about fifteen feet from the opening of the first tent and we could see the back of Gaddafi. It was actually his side profile. He was sitting in a chair about a foot up, almost like he was on a throne. Below him was an elderly Libyan gentleman, talking in Arabic and waving his hands. While I watched I noticed Gaddafi didn't move. No facial expressions. You know how when you're talking you make some kind of a movement after a while, right? It was a setup. I guess it was either a wax figure of him or a damn good plastic one. The profile looked just like him.

I said to the guy next to me, "Don't do anything stupid." I was sure they had night vision out there behind one of those sand dunes and there were guns focused on our heads.

I told my companion, "It's just a little test. It's no big deal. That's not Gaddafi. We're being tested right now." The guy was getting kind of nervous. It was probably the longest two minutes ever for both of us.

Finally, a gentleman came over and said, "Oman Muntasir is waiting for you with Colonel Gaddafi." We understood and followed him to another tent.

And there was Oman Muntasir, Colonel Gaddafi and an older gentleman making tea. He asked us to sit down, which we did. Oman Muntasir was his interpreter—his only interpreter—and the only one allowed in the tent other than the guy pouring tea for us. Through Muntasir we talked. I was told that Gaddafi understood some English but always used a translator. It gave him a chance to think and look at you while you were talking.

Gaddafi told us how terrible the United States of America was. How several years back, during the Reagan administration, we killed his adopted eight-year-old daughter.

I said, "Colonel Gaddafi, I never heard that in the press."

"Yes, your F-15 fighters flew in to bomb and kill me," he said. "They flew so low that people could even see the pilots. They blew up what they thought was my Palace and my eight-year-old adopted daughter was in it."

"Colonel Gaddafi, sir," I said. "With all due respect, I want to apologize on behalf of the entire American public. I'm sure we didn't know about it. I don't even know if President Reagan knew about it. I apologize. That's terrible. I'm sure we were trying to kill you, not your eight-year-old daughter. I'm so sorry."

As I said all this, the people around me were getting a little nervous. Colonel Gaddafi looked me in the eye and there was silence for about five seconds. Of course, when you're in a scene like that, it feels like a lot longer.

Then he said something in Arabic while I held my breath. Then Omar Muntasir translated, "Nobody from the West ever apologized for that. It's the first time anyone's ever apologized. Thank you very much."

Whew! Acting like one considerate human being to another made a difference. Then I said, "Colonel Gaddafi, one of the reasons I'm here is as a good citizen of the world. I'm not an agent of the CIA or the FBI or any agency."

He answered, "I know who you are. I know what you have done to help out others."

"Sir," I went on, "what kind of verification of your agreement with the West can I help with? It would be great to get this done, because then you could trade with our country, which I know you want to do. Please tell me how we can settle on the two suspected terrorists."

"Number one, will they be tried in The Hague," he asked, "or will they be intercepted by MI6 or a special operations force and be forced to go on trial in England or Scotland?"

I said, "Sir, I can guarantee you this. They will go on trial in The Hague. And if they don't, I will go to the press of the world and tell them that you have been totally cheated and lied to. You know I can do that. And I want nothing in return."

He said, "If you pull this off and if it works the way you say it will, I will give you fifty million dollars."

"Colonel Gaddafi, thank you, but I'm sure you've checked me out. As you know, I have my own money. I'm not here for the money, sir. I'm here for peace, love, and happiness. That's all I'm here for. I don't want anything in return."

He looked surprised. "No one's ever said that. Many people come to me for money, for millions to make this happen, and it never happens. What do you want then?"

"How about this? After everything goes back to normal again, maybe in a year or two, I'll fly in with my family and we'll have dinner with your family? How's that?"

Done.

The next thing is quite interesting. He said, "Number two, can the two men eat the same way they eat here?"

I was confused. "Colonel Gaddafi, I've been here for three days, waiting for you. I love your food. It's Mediterranean food. You know, I'm part Greek."

He said, "We prepare our food a certain way."

"Well, sir, can you give me an idea, because I've been eating the best food. What's different?"

He asked Omar Muntasir to explain, which he did. "We slaughter animals similar to the Jewish people. You know, the way they slaughter and prepare their food."

I had a tickle bone in me and broke out laughing. Muntasir's mouth dropped, Gaddafi looked like he wanted to kill me, and Jerry, the gentleman next to me, was equally surprised and silent. There was this unbelievable pause with a look on everyone's face like what the heck are you doing? Maybe four seconds went by so I said, "Colonel Gaddafi, you and the Jews have not liked each other all these years, right? You don't get along. But you eat exactly alike. Isn't that funny?" And I laughed again.

Then his angry look turned into a smile, and he said, "Yes. Yes, that is funny."

I had an eight-dollar camera in my pocket, one of those throwaway cameras I'd bought in Tunisia. "Can we take a picture?" I asked.

He said, "Yes."

I gave the camera to Omar Muntasir, and he took several pictures of me and Gaddafi. I still have those pictures.

Colonel Gaddafi and Me in Libya
Photo courtesy of author's personal collection

Afterwards, they flew me to Tunisia on one of their medical planes. I boarded that little jet that was sitting there to get me back to London. When we got back to the United States, I shared my experience with Washington. And I was very quiet about it. I never did any press releases. I was able to help get him to release the two suspected terrorists of Pan Am Flight 103. Within three months, those two suspected terrorists went on trial in The Hague. One was found guilty, and one was acquitted. I never did get back for that dinner.

Chapter 22
"I'll Have a Side of That"

Sometimes the projects I get involved in have a big effect on a particular population, or even the world. Sometimes they're just for fun. I suppose someone could argue I changed their world with Patrón (which I sold in 2018), but that's kind of a stretch. I can afford to play with things like that just because they make me happy. And I'm not talking about the money. We all need things in our life that just make us happy.

I get asked all the time to do things. People ask for money, my time, my expertise. Of course, JP's Peace, Love & Happiness Family Foundation screens anything that comes to me that is humanitarian-related. But with businesses, and yes, even some government agencies, I'll get involved in a lot of different things, mostly how to be a more effective, kinder manager, which affects efficiency of an organization. I speak and get involved with grammar schools, high schools, and universities. I've held classes with Yale, Pepperdine, Stanford, Rice, University of Texas, and USC, to name a few. Sometimes I get an idea for a solution and go out searching for it. Other times, we'll create something to fill a need.

Side gigs are something I've also done, like being the Executive Producer of *Sound of Freedom, Kiss the Ground* and *Common Ground* and others. I didn't do things like this when I was starting to build Paul Mitchell, but now I love to do things that are good and influential.

Bandero

I'm back in the alcohol business again. Tequila is one of my passions and I wanted to do something new and different. My new tequila is Bandero, and it's made in the tequila region of Jalisco, Mexico, using the finest agave. Bandero is a very smooth tequila, it leaves you with a warmth at the back of your throat. We're hoping it will appeal to men and women in a way that other tequilas don't. Nobody else is doing anything like it right now.

I actually started Bandero with my friend, JK, and to date we've done very little promotion. For a while the name was on the top fuel race car driven by my daughter, Alexis. We've grown mostly by word of mouth. And I've started to personally promote the brand.

And by the way, Bandero has already won eight Gold medals in the tequila juice and packaging! We even won the Gold medal in 2024 from Mexico as one of the best tasting tequilas in Mexico.

Round 2 Spirits, LLC (Blue Weber Agave Vodka)

One of the geniuses of Patrón was our CEO, Ed Brown. After our non-compete was up, he had the brilliant idea to get our old executive team back again and start a different kind of vodka. This one is not made out of corn or wheat or rye or potatoes. It's the first one to be made out of one-hundred percent Blue Weber Agave.

Because it's made out of agave, I'm told that your insulin does not spike as happens with many other vodkas. And it's the first ever certified additive-free vodka. Almost all other alcohols (besides high-end tequila) can be more of a downer or depressant. It's gluten-free, and it has fewer calories than other vodkas. Those are the key things that make it unique and different.

Thanks to Ed Brown and our team's connections, we have started this new company and are already seeing very successful results in many states. Ed Brown is my dear friend and he and our team are geniuses in the field.

Sound of Freedom

I never thought I'd be in the movie business, but I made a recent and unexpected investment and it was an adventure. It all started about five years ago, when my friend Eduardo came to visit. Eduardo is a Mexican actor who did the voiceover of Jesus in the Spanish version of *Son of God* which came out in 2013. He's an amazing fellow and a good buddy of mine. He has his own production company, and its goal is not just to entertain, but to make a difference in society.

We were watching my daughter Alexis race on TV—a race she won. While we were celebrating, Eduardo told me about a DEA agent trying to stop child trafficking in foreign countries. He thought the government wasn't doing enough. They wouldn't let him cross the border to bust these people. So, he left.

What did he do next? He got a group together of law enforcement and they all went down to Colombia to put together a sting operation. According to Eduardo, the group worked to convince some children sex traffickers that they were traffickers too and wanted to buy all their kids. A couple dozen of the traffickers and transporters showed up and brought with them about forty little boys and girls that they were selling for sex. I mean these were children, little kids. The former agent and his group busted every one of them. They even got the Colombian government involved.

Eduardo wanted to make a movie about it and told me about his plans. The movie would show everything about what these traffickers were doing. The film would show how they'd talk parents into releasing their kids for a photo shoot and then never return them. And it would reveal how they'd con people, how they'd take the children and hide them, and how they'd transport the kids. He had an unbelievable vision for the movie.

Then Eduardo came to me and shared his dilemma. "JP, I'm having problems. There's a lot of people interested, but don't want to invest because it's too controversial."

I've known Eduardo for years. He's an honest man. I said, "Eduardo, when you told me about your film, goosebumps ran down my arm. Your movie has got to be made." So, I gave him one million on the spot. "Here's your first million," I said. "You go talk to some of the same people you talked to before and say, 'JP just put in the first million.'" Within a few months, he raised all the rest of money.

He started making the movie in 2018 and shopped it for three years after it was done. He went to every big studio and even went to online streaming movie channels. Everyone told him they were interested but never got back to him. He did manage to show it himself at a few places, but it looked as if it would die on the vine. What you need to know about Eduardo is that he's a religious man and he was praying. He also told his friends and followers, "Please pray to God to send me an angel to help out somehow. We've got to get this movie out." He was a very determined man because it was such a good cause.

His prayers were answered. One day out of the blue, he got a phone call from Angel Studios. That's right—Angel Studios! They are located in Provo, Utah. I think the owners may have only done a few films in their entire life. They said "Look, we're really behind this. We saw your film and we'd like a shot at putting it out." Eduardo figured he had nothing to lose. Why not?

Anyway, within three months, they had it scheduled for release in two thousand theaters. It was the Fourth of July weekend. *Indiana Jones and the Dial of Destiny* was being released the same weekend, and the latest *Mission Impossible* movie was coming out in another week or so. They told him it was a good time because a lot of people wouldn't be able to get in to see the big studio releases. They'd have a good shot at those turned away going to Eduardo's movie instead.

There was little to no advertising budget. It hit the screen in 2,000 theaters without any real promotion. *Indiana Jones* was in 4,500 theaters and Eduardo's movie, *Sound of Freedom* beat it, breaking records. It made Angel Studios the first ever to see a second week jump of more than thirty-five percent during the summer season. We did over fourteen million its first day. In its first few weeks, we did over forty million. Two days later, it was on Fox News. They did a ten-minute special with the star of the movie on why it was so unique. In the end, *Sound of Freedom* made over a quarter of a million dollars, and I believe has made it into the Top 10 highest-grossing independent films..

Training the CIA and the FBI

It's not a secret that I trained for the CIA on more than one occasion. Subject: Management Motivation. It made the front page of the *Wall Street Journal* at the end of the 1990s. The article read, "Have a nice hair day at the CIA. John Paul DeJoria of Paul Mitchell trains the agents on how to be a more loving, kind manager."

After 9/11 they called me again. There were issues. The FBI and CIA weren't sharing enough information to each other. Everyone was demoralized, and the country was in shock. George Tenet, the Director of the CIA, through Buzzy Krongard, the Executive Director, reached out to me. "JP, would you mind talking to our CIA staff about dealing with change?"

I said, "Sure."

I flew back to Washington D.C. on my own nickel. Again, I'm not an agent. They know I'm an American citizen who loves our country and wants to do the right thing. I met them at the CIA headquarters in Langley, Virginia and went into an area called the bubble. The bubble is a big room for eight or nine hundred people, and it's completely shut off from everything else. I trained them on how to deal with change.

The first thing I told them was that you cannot change yesterday's newspaper. I continued, "I don't care what you do or say, you cannot change it. But if you look at yesterday's bad news as an example of what went wrong, you may be able to see how you can keep it from happening again." We learned a giant lesson when the World Trade Center towers went down. Analyzing the past will help you avoid making the same mistakes in the future.

"What's the best way to do that?" I asked. "Get everyone involved. Not just the people on the front line. Talk with the

FBI, the State Department, and others in the CIA. Talk with the people on the ground as well as their administrators. Let everyone talk freely in the same room. I know your agencies often compete with each other and don't share information. But getting everyone involved is the only way to go."

A.B. 'Buzzy' Krongard, Executive Director of CIA, and John Anthony, Eloise, and Me; This was when John Anthony received his special Agent 006½ badge

Photo courtesy of author's personal collection, received from Executive Director Krongard.

After that, their younger, upper-echelon staff came in for another meeting with me and we covered the same thing. My wife Eloise and our son John Anthony had come with me and were not allowed to attend the sessions. Eloise and John Anthony were entertained in the director's office while they waited. They took Eloise and John Anthony for a tour of the CIA Museum which was so exciting for my little boy. I think he was about four years old at the time.

To thank me for coming, they took all three of us into a special room of the CIA so we could see how the United States is keeping its eye on the happenings of the world. John Anthony set off alarms because he was the only one without a badge. Then George Tenet had a special badge made for him. It said Agent 006½. We still have that badge today.

I also trained the FBI on more than one occasion. My friend and special agent, Don C., had me do lectures on kindness in management, motivation, and staff retention.

Me, Eloise, and Buzzy Krongard, Executive Director CIA

Chapter 23

At Home

I'm calling this chapter "At Home" because I wanted to give you a taste of what the other side of my life is like. I don't separate my business from my personal life. It's all the same and I love it all, but I haven't talked about it much. Let's start with my family. You've already met my mother and brother, two of the most amazing people I've ever known. They're no longer with us, but I have a lot of wonderful memories.

My Brother, Bobby

You met my brother and best friend, Robert Anthony DeJoria, early in the book. He was eighteen months older than I am. Having him with me when we were in foster care made a big difference during those years. With him there, I had piece of home with me all the time. He was the best friend anyone could ever have. We hung out together most of the time. I loved him dearly.

My brother was the first entrepreneur in the family. It was in his blood. He started the first photocopy machine service in Beverly Hills. He was the first to get a Xerox machine and start a little business. He charged people four cents a copy at his place on Little Santa Monica Boulevard in Beverly Hills. Then he branched out and started another one in Culver

City. He was about twenty-eight years old when he died in a motorcycle accident. He was a great brother, and he was respected by everyone.

I miss him dearly, but his characteristics are reflected in the personality of my niece Heather.

My Mother, Yvonne

My mother you've also met. Her name was Yvonne DeJoria. My mom was a superstar. She was a ballroom dancer even into her nineties. She was one of the most positive human beings on the planet. She'd look at something as a challenge, never a problem. I remember one time in my early twenties when we were having Thanksgiving dinner at her house. She had the table set for eight people because we had some friends with no place to go. Then, she said, "I bet you have other friends that don't have family here. Why don't you invite them too? I don't care how many there are. We're going to feed them."

There turned out to be over twenty people in her house that day. She put chairs between chairs and got out the old TV tray tables we used when I was kid. Somehow, she made enough to go around for everybody. That's the kind of loving person she was. Years later, when she learned that I had been homeless, she was so upset. She told me if I hadn't been so proud, I could have stayed with her. For sure, things would have been a lot easier! She also loved coming to our Paul Mitchell seminars. She'd ask me when our next seminar was and plan her life around it. When she got there, everyone wanted to be around her. I loved her beyond words and am grateful for her positive influence. It still drives me today.

**Me & mom on a motorcycle at a Paul Mitchell event in Hawaii;
Mom was always up for fun adventures!**

From Luke Jacobellis

JP's mom, Yvonne, was at every Paul Mitchell event. She was a very active lady, and she was a dancer. At our parties, JP would always have the first dance with her, and she would always have the best seat in the house. He would make sure to recognize her in front of the crowd and he'd make sure my wife took special care of her when he was busy with other responsibilities. JP was the perfect son. He didn't just pay attention to her; he loved and respected her. He made her the center of attention at every event, whether it was a gathering or Christmas party.

From Alexis DeJoria

My grandmother was a very humble, sweet, incredible woman. When my grandfather went off to war, she was left alone with two boys. She worked two jobs, just to have them home on weekends. You'd never know she had any hardships in her life. She was always appreciative and never complained.

My Wife, Eloise

I'll admit it. In the marriage area I've made a lot of mistakes, probably because I started off too young. I never gave up though because I'm a positive person. It took a while, but I met my perfect match in 1991 and never looked back. We met on a blind date.

Sometimes things happen in the most serendipitous ways. That's the story of how Eloise and I were introduced. A girl (I think her name was Wendon) met each of us separately over a two-week period. For reasons I'll never understand, she thought we would be a good match and took it upon herself to make the introduction. She reached out to me and said, "I met this girl a few weeks ago. You guys have similar personalities. You're both happy-go-lucky people and you've got to meet each other." She gave me her name and number and I promised to call. What I didn't know was she had said the same thing to Eloise.

I was traveling at the time and when I called, Eloise knew a little about me. We had a great conversation about our children, and she seemed like the nicest person. We made a date for brunch. When we finally met, sparks started flying on both sides. And we never made it to brunch. But the story gets better!

It seemed that her friends Ron and Lisa wanted to introduce us six months earlier, but Eloise wasn't ready then. When she finally told them she was ready to meet me, Ron said, "It's too late. He's gone. He doesn't stay single very long. There's no way in the world he's not with somebody right now." So, instead of going to brunch, we drove up to Ron and Lisa's ranch to say hello and show them we'd met. We haven't been separated since.

You might think I'm crazy, but I'd made a list of everything I wanted in a woman back then. I showed it to Eloise, then ripped it up and threw it away. Not only was she everything on that list, but she was also a couple of things I'd forgotten to write down!

Eloise is a gem and she's been an asset to JPMS too. In 1992, she became a corporate spokesmodel for the business. Her beautiful face and hair were in almost every ad we did for the next twenty-five years. But Eloise is way more than a beautiful face. She's a great mom and a great companion. We often travel together, and she always knows exactly what to do and say. She went with me to New York when I received a seat on the New York Stock Exchange from Mr. Dick Grasso. She's a great ambassador for the events I go to or the dinners I have with celebrities. Just yesterday we talked about a recent trip and how grateful we were for the people we met and everything we learned. We live a beautiful life.

Eloise & Me at the Selfless Love gala
Photo courtesy of Selfless Love and Ashley Brown

———— ✳ ————

From Eloise DeJoria

I couldn't believe how positive John Paul was. At first, I thought this man is not real. But he is real. We've been together many decades and he's still the same. He's an action person and he's one hundred percent giving all day long. That's his MO. John Paul also mixes his business with his personal life. On our first date we went to our friend Ron's house, and he carried a bottle of Patrón in his hand. He wanted them to try his new product.

I remember when he showed me the list of everything he wanted in a girl. It was so worn you could tell it had been opened and closed a lot. He had everything down there, even the height. I thought I was all those things on the list, but I wasn't going to tell him that. If anyone else had given me a list I might have been upset. But he was so kind and sweet, and his heart was in such a good place. From that moment, I guess I started to fall in love with him.

John Paul was like my knight in shining armor. Here I was, a working mother who'd been doing a bit of modeling. With JP it literally felt like Doris Day and Rock Hudson. Then he asked me to be the face of Paul Mitchell, and I got to work with such incredible photographers such as Richard Avedon, Annie Leibowitz, Herb Ritts, Norman Jean Roy, Steven Lipman, etc. We went all around the world for Paul Mitchell, and he was building his business the whole time. I think the fact that he was using his wife as the face of his company really resonated with women.

My father always cared about the planet, so when John Paul got into philanthropy, my dream was to do it side by side with him. Helping people who need support makes me feel good too. And I have my own charities. I was very lost when I was young. Helping young girls who've been abused to become strong and independent makes me feel so good inside.

I've learned so much living with John Paul. He's so full of hope and possibilities. He works hard all day long, whether it's with his businesses or his charities. He never stops believing that being positive and focused and putting good energy into something will work out in the end.

Eloise and Me in a JPMS campaign

Photo courtesy of John Paul Mitchell Systems (photographer: Takashi Kitamura)

Now let me introduce you to my children. They are all great kids.

John Paul II—Oldest Son

John Paul is that terrific kid I told you about who was with me during the early years before JPMS. With all the help I got back then from my mom, those amazing biker ladies, and other friends, you could say he was raised by a village. His name is John Paul DeJoria II, named after me but he has always been his own person, and he still is today. He went through a lot of challenges in his life . . . but came out on top. When he graduated from high school, we went on an adventure to Spain and Tangiers together, great bonding and fun.

Me and John Paul II
Photo courtesy of author's personal collection

That little boy became a true entrepreneur. He has a great cannabis-type coffee shop in Oregon which features music and entertainment. It's legal up there. He also has a vineyard and a bed and breakfast business. Most importantly, he has some terrific kids. My granddaughter, John's eldest daughter, graduated at the top of her class from Cornell and is now excelling in sales and business. Another grandchild is finishing at Cornell right now, with a master's in hospitality. I'm so pleased with what John has done of his life. He may have had a rough start, but today he has his own business and raised some of the best children. Another grandchild is in the beauty industry and another grandchild, believe it or not, John Paul III, gave me two beautiful great-grandchildren. What more could a father want?

Alexis and Me when she won the US Nationals in Indy
Photo courtesy of author's personal collection

Alexis DeJoria—Oldest Daughter

Alexis came along next, and is a wonderful, gracious, giving lady. By the way, she's also a champion race car driver. She drives a Top Fuel Funny Car. Those are some of the fastest cars in the world. How fast do they go? From a dead stop to 336 miles an hour in 3.88 seconds. Oh yeah—she's fast. One of the fastest in the world. In 2014, she won the NHRA (National Hot Rod Association) US Nationals in Indianapolis on Labor Day. It was a big upset. First, because she's the only female driver left in the Funny Car category. Second, because every other car ran really well and she still outraced everyone else. Her ultimate goal is to become the overall Funny Car world champion. I think she's going to make it!

It's probably not a surprise that Alexis loves motorcycles and has ridden with me at times, even on long trips. One of our rides was a two-day drive from Livingston, Montana with Peter Fonda, Robbie Knievel, Bill Shaffer, and C. B. Sullivan. We arrived two days later in Sturgis, South Dakota where I received the biker Hall of Fame award, which sits in their museum. I had so much biker fun with my daughter. She also shares my passion for environmental conservation and animal protection. She's the first one who turned me on to Paul Watson's work to protect whales, seals, and other marine life. We served together for one week with Captain Paul Watson on his Sea Shepherd ship in the Bay of Saint Lawrence, Canada, to protect baby harp seals from being clubbed to death for their furs. Watson said that we saved at least 100,000 baby harp seals from being destroyed.

Me and Alexis in Bay of St. Laurence, Canada, working with Captain Paul Watson to save baby Harp seals

Photo courtesy of author's personal collection

Alexis is a giver too. She's fundraised for cancer awareness, especially breast and pancreatic cancers. She's also provided me with a beautiful granddaughter. I'm honored to call Alexis my daughter.

From Alexis

I was very shy when I was young, but I soon became the wild child of the family. I'd get up in the middle of the night and ride my tricycle around the house and into their bed. When I was five, I wanted to be a fighter pilot. But once I started high school, I knew I wanted to race cars. My first car was a 1993 GMC Typhoon. Before I could buy anything, it had to meet all of his criteria. My dad said it had to be used, a good-sized car and a reasonable price. They only made them for a few years and it was in good condition. It was also kind of big. Dad had no idea. One of his close friends, Clint Eastwood, had just sold the same car he'd bought because it was too fast and not safe cornering! I remember driving back from Long Beach with my dad and after hearing Clint Eastwood's story, he said, "Oh my God, I just bought you a race car!"

I went to my first drag race when I was sixteen. I was still in high school, and it was the first time I saw one of those Funny Cars go down. That was it. I thought, "One day I will be driving that car." College wasn't for me, and I worked at JPMS for four years, but I had that itch at the back of my mind. My dad always says, "If you can make your passion your profession, then you're going to be successful." So, he agreed to let me go out and try it. Of course, he didn't expect me to come back with a license to race.

Within eight months I was winning races, but I had no history in racing, so I had to start at the bottom and learn the ropes. As a side note, I feel pretty good about the fact that I'm the only one in the family that has access to all of dad's cars and motorcycles.

When we were growing up, my father was gone a lot on business trips. He was trying to build up the company. But when he was home, he was home. It was like the best thing ever. He was a very good father. When I had my own child, I'd remember certain things he said or certain ways he would act and especially around his grandchildren. I strive to be that kind of person.

When it comes to life and racing, I'm very competitive. And my father's like, "Oh, it doesn't matter if you didn't qualify. At least you tried." I try not to get stuck in my pity party so I can become the best person I can be.

Although I was a single child with half siblings, I never knew them to be anything else but a full sister or brother. He worked really hard to keep us involved, to make sure we knew that he loved us.

He took me on quite a few business trips with him and I would have the best time ever. Once I went out on this eighty-foot sailboat called "Oceans of Fantasy" with him and his crew. I was about eight. We sailed through the Caribbean and slept in hammocks on the deck, and it was the coolest thing ever. I used to sit all the way up on the very tippy, tippy front of the bow with my legs dangling in the water. To me it was an adventure.

My father has such a giving, loving heart, and he has so much energy! My dad lives a good peaceful life. He's always giving, and some people take advantage of him but he doesn't get jaded. He still has an open heart and never holds a grudge. He's also very spontaneous. That's because he's so in the moment. I could go on and on about my father. He's been an integral part of my life. I've tried to emulate things I've seen him do. He's just a good, kind man, and I would do anything for him.

———— ❊ ————

Me and Michaeline, riding on the back of our 'Patrón Express' train

Photo courtesy of author's personal collection

Michaeline—Youngest Daughter

Michaeline is my youngest daughter and a genius, in my opinion. She's always been very smart. One year she helped me plan a father/daughter vacation to Europe with her and Alexis. It was a great trip . . . so much fun . . . and she was six years old! She skipped grades early on and graduated from college at twenty-two with two degrees. When she began working at JPMS I suggested she start as a receptionist and learn the various parts of the company.

"No, Dad," she said to me. "I'm not going to start as a receptionist. I'm going to start in the warehouse. If I'm going to take your place as CEO one day, I need to learn every single job first."

I reminded her that I would never retire and would always remain Chairman of the Board. She said, "I know that dad. But I'm younger than you are. I'll outlive you!"

So, she started in the warehouse, packing boxes and shipping, and had almost every job in the company over time. She worked her way up and took over the company as CEO about four years ago. Our company continues to grow. She is so capable and giving. (By the way, I'm still Chairman of the Board.) Michaeline is a perfect mother to three amazing and gifted children. I am proud.

———— ❈ ————

From Michaeline

My father is fully and completely himself to all people at all times. With him, there's no environment where he tends to be more or less of anything. He will show the same respect and kindness to a king as he will to a cab driver. There's no shapeshifting. He looks at the world through a lens of beauty and of gratitude, not of self-serving or mindless thinking. He has a really heightened awareness of the world around him. He genuinely feels blessed to be able to touch lives. I've talked to his old friends, and he was the same way in middle school. He was just nice and kind to everybody. Back then he had nothing to give back but his energy. In a way, he's always been philanthropic, even before he had money. Giving his energy back is really special.

One of my favorite stories about him was at a family dinner at a restaurant in Malibu. I was probably eight or nine and we ended up talking and staying up way too late. My dad was friends with the owner, so they were cool with our still being there. It was probably midnight and the restaurant had been closed for about a half hour. The servers had cleaned up and one of them cranked the music up. When that music started, we were dancing all around that restaurant. We laughed and we lived and we had a great time. No one suggested we go to bed. It was life presenting us with an opportunity to be joyful together. It seems like a simple memory, right? But it was so much more than that. It was symbolic of how my dad lives.

My dad is such a positive person.

He was always positive when I was growing up. I never once heard my dad say negative things about me. I was a genius. I was the greatest person in life. I was magical. I was born a crystal child with an elevated vibration, who just got things that other people didn't. If I'd told him I wanted to be an underwater basket weaver, he would have said, "Mikee, you're going to be the best underwater basket weaver the world has ever seen."

So, I grew up thinking I can be anything I want and be amazing at it—because I'm this elevated creature. And apparently, I'm a genius! I never searched for something to make myself whole because I was raised to believe that I was already whole. I saw how much passion and enthusiasm my dad had for what he did. It was as if I sipped the Kool-Aid in utero. I wanted what he had too.

———— ✳ ————

John Anthony—Youngest Son

My youngest son, John Anthony, is another very smart kid. I'm lucky I ended up with some pretty smart kids. And their personalities are just great. The good Lord has blessed me in that way. He gave them good beings in their bodies. John Anthony is a child of Eloise and me. He's a full-blown entrepreneur in the agricultural business and doing extremely well. He currently runs three different companies.

He traveled many parts of the world with me on business . . . and adventures with me and his mom. He brought back to classmates a report on his adventures and things to do in other countries, how they lived, money they spent, their religion, their government, etc. We climbed Mount Kilimanjaro to the top to see the sunrise as he turned eighteen years old—a magical experience.

He is honest, tells you like it is, and is very caring about others.

———— ☀ ————

From John Anthony

I've been learning so much about agriculture in the last couple of years, putting a lot of emphasis on regenerative growing and trying to do everything in a conscientious way. I got hooked on it when I was younger and Pops would take me on trips around the world. He always wanted to know what was going on with his other companies, not just Paul Mitchell and Patrón. As a result, I saw a lot of farms, manufacturing and mining operations, a whole cool side of things that you don't really get to see as a kid. I learned that I liked to spend my time outside in the sun, near plants and crops.

**John Anthony and Me on his 18th birthday as we climbed
to the top of Mt. Kilimanjaro**

Photos courtesy of author's personal collection

*When I turned eighteen, I wanted to climb the Seven
Summits, starting with Kilimanjaro. Pops decided to join me for
my birthday. He was seventy-two and I was turning eighteen. I
was like, "Dad, I really wanted to do this on my own. I feel this
is a rite of passage journey."*

And my dad said, "Son, let's do this together."

I fought it at first. I really wanted it to be on my own on a journey of self-discovery.

I'm really happy it didn't turn out that way, since we ended up doing a lot of really cool stuff together. We drove deep into the Serengeti plains during the Great Migration. I'd never been around so many living creatures in one place. We saw millions of wildebeests and zebras all around us in these massive valleys. It was like taking in life at its full spectrum. We went into these crazy rivers and ravines where fifteen-to-twenty-foot crocodiles (they called them flying dragons) jumped from the tops of riverbanks, catching the animals down below. It was as if they were feeding their way through the Great Migration.

We went deep into the heart of Tanzania and saw coffee farms, chili pepper farms, lots of other farms as we got acclimated leading up to the climb. Then we did Kilimanjaro together. It took us seven days to go up, with my dad leading the way. What a brutal hike on that last day. We woke up before midnight and hiked for six hours to make it up to the summit by sunrise. The air was so thin we could barely breathe up there in the freezing cold. Then we had to hike another ten or twelve hours down to the first base camp. I was faster going downhill because it was easier on my knees. It took us seven days to go up and one day to go down.

Through the whole trip he told me more stories about his childhood than he ever had before. My dad's early life was tough, but he always believed that things would turn out okay, as long as you stick with it. He's a complete optimist. He also treats everyone with equal respect. I've seen him meet with people on the streets and with kings, queens, and heads of state. The way he interacts with people doesn't change. He also has endless curiosity. He barely knows how to use a smartphone, but he's curious about artificial intelligence, archeology, biology, even aliens, to name a few. And he always wants to know how he can make a difference, how he can help. He also has one extraordinary talent: his objectivity. Through practice and mindset, he's been able to master where he puts the energy in his body. When he gets mad, he just takes that energy and puts it into generating positive ideas or outcomes. He's very good at objectively diverting energy into places where it matters most. If somebody wants to learn how to emulate his style, I think that's the bread and butter of it.

Those are my four kids. I also have two stepsons. But before I tell you more about them, I'd like to introduce you to someone who comes to our home almost every day and has become a part of our family for many years.

Our Personal Chef

His name is Judd Servidio. He's been with us for seventeen years and he's one of the most fabulous human beings on the planet. He's also our personal chef. Eloise discovered Judd one time when I was traveling out of town.

We had a few people coming over and our optometrist said to her, "Why don't you try this chef? You guys are hiring cooks all the time. You should try this one. You'll really like him." He explained that Judd did styling work where he took pictures of food for magazines but in addition, he was a really good chef. So, Eloise hired him for a couple of days.

Afterwards, she called me and said, "Sweetheart, you've got to taste this guy's food."

As soon as I got back, I tasted his food and that was it.

"Do you want a happy job?" I asked. "You want to work for us?" I didn't hesitate. "You're hired."

He's been with us ever since. I think he's one of the greatest chefs on the planet. I don't think I've ever tasted the same meal twice. And he has a book out called, *Salt and Vanilla: A Cook's Book of Edible Art with Stories.* His wife and kids are like family. They're great, positive people to be around. Judd and his family are the best.

Although I'll never forget the one time he failed us. It was Thanksgiving and we were at our home in Colorado. Judd wanted to be with his family so he prepared dinner ahead of time. There were plenty of side dishes and the turkey was ready to go in the oven. All we had to do was put it in and take it out at the right time. We did everything Judd told us to do and everything was perfect except for one big problem. We couldn't find the stuffing. There was none in the turkey. We thought, maybe he put it in a side dish, but no luck. It was Thanksgiving and there wasn't any stuffing? What was Judd doing to us? I mean you can't have Thanksgiving without stuffing! It was definitely an emergency.

So, of course I called him. "Where's the stuffing?"

Judd said he didn't make any stuffing.

"Why not?" I asked. "It's Thanksgiving. We always have stuffing at Thanksgiving."

Judd gave us some crazy answer about Eloise being on a no bread kick at the time and there were only three of us and he'd prepared a big spread for us so he didn't think we'd miss it.

That was the first and last Thanksgiving we had no stuffing. He made sure of it. Otherwise, Judd is a great guy, a great guy!

From Judd Servidio

Working for JP and Eloise as their personal chef has been a wonderful experience. I've worked with Michelin chefs and for countless celebrities and business executives but working for JP is the best. They've given me the freedom and ability to continue my creativity. Being creative is what drives me. JP and Eloise can eat anywhere in the world and have the best of the best. So, I'm always mentally challenging myself. It's as if I'm competing with some of the best restaurants in the world.

At first, I worked for JP part time. When he said, "Why don't we go full time," I wasn't sure, so I asked for a contract.

"We don't do contracts," he said.

"I've been building up my reputation in Austin," I told him. "What if you don't want me after a year and I have to start all over again?"

"We've got employees that have been with us twenty or thirty years," he answered. "Don't worry about it. We'll take care of you."

I said, "Okay. I'll go with that." And I've been with them over fifteen years now.

There's a kind of hierarchy in most high net worth homes. Employees are treated in a business-like way. In some cases, the chef doesn't even talk to the client. He or she has to go through a manager. John Paul and Eloise aren't like that. He treats us like family. My family has stayed in their guest house in Colorado and their home in LA, and they've invited us to fly on their plane multiple times. I'm not treated like the help, the way it is in other places. I guess that's one of the reasons why our relationship has lasted so long.

I'm sure he told you the Thanksgiving story. We have an arrangement that I do Christmas for them and Thanksgiving with my own family in Austin. I had everything set up for them in Colorado. If I recall, it was only the three of them: John Paul, Eloise, and John Anthony. Eloise wasn't eating any bread at this point, and I made seven or eight different dishes to go with the turkey. There was plenty of other food so I thought I could get away with one less thing. The next day I get a call and they're like "Where's the stuffing?" I was so wrong. Now it's a running joke. Every year at Thanksgiving someone always says, "I hope there'll be stuffing this year." Needless to say, I haven't forgotten the stuffing since.

There's so much about JP that I admire. He always looks at the positive in life. I try to do the best I can, but he's at another level. He's had many business failures in his life and people taking advantage of him, but he always rises above it. There are so many stories about the good he's done. I've gone with him to Mobile Loaves & Fishes and we've cooked for the people there. Of course, he's given them money for things they've built, including an automotive shop and an entrepreneurial business center. He sees a need and he fills it.

He inspired me during COVID to pitch in myself. We'd make four to five hundred meals for all the hospital workers. John Paul and Eloise would pay for the food, then help me put it together and pass the meals out to all the workers. He told me, "I'm proud of you for doing this because you're not looking for anything in return."

I said, "You've kind of set an example and we have the means to do it, so why not?" I'll sometimes make their Thanksgiving meal on the Wednesday before, and they might help at a soup kitchen on the actual holiday. They don't just give out their

money, they also give their time. It's an example anybody can take from.

Michael Harvey

I also have two stepsons. Michael Harvey is Eloise's oldest son. He is starting a spa business with his wife, Semia, who's been in the industry for a while. He is my go-to guy to get answers on so many things. He's a great computer geek.

Michael is a great stepson, and he has very good, smart and happy children. He is very respectful and appreciated.

Justin Harvey

Justin Harvey is Eloise's younger son. He's about Alexis's age and another entrepreneur. I gave him a little helping hand to get into the recovery business. He has a place called The Arbor near Austin, Texas. It's probably the number one recovery place in the world. I say that because a solid percentage of people don't have to return. Recovery—whether it's from alcohol, drugs, or an emotional problem—is like a revolving door. You're in, you're out, and then you're in again. Back and forth. Back and forth. Justin's place has found a way to up the odds on recovery.

Later, with Gary Stephens, we started Renew Logic to recycle electronics and reuse and redistribute overstocks or returns from major companies.

Justin and his wife, Wendy, are great parents and have three beautiful daughters. He's a really good person and I'm proud of what he's done.

From Justin Harvey

Before my mother married John Paul, I went through a pretty rough time. Thanks to them, I finally got my life straightened out and could see light at the end of the tunnel. John Paul saw that in me and said, "Man, you're a changed human being. I would like to offer you the chance to start a business."

It's important to understand that John Paul has instilled his value system in all of his children, and I consider myself one of his children, even though I'm a step-child. He was a self-made person who worked from the bottom up. Even though he empowers us to take that first step, he expects us to work for our goals. I experienced his ability to forgive and forget and to love unconditionally. He saw talent and hope in me, and he invested in that. He empowered me to become something beyond what I was. At first, it scared me to death.

I'd been sober for about a year and had started working in the treatment industry, but I didn't know what kind of business I wanted to start. Then it was suggested to me that I start doing what I love which was treating people who needed help. I had a broad understanding of what good treatment would look like, but I had no idea how to go about it. So, I hired Jim Walker, who is now my partner. Jim has been in the business for over thirty five years, had run another facility in Texas, and understood the whole industry. We went to John Paul to present our business plan. He approved our initial loan which allowed us to start an in-patient drug and alcohol rehab, from furniture to staffing to licensure to every single thing in place. We accomplished that in less than a year.

My partner and I paid John Paul back during our first ten years of business. It was a pretty amazing accomplishment. And he's always telling me, "You're probably one of the few that have paid me back—one hundred percent! I feel honored that he put his trust in me.

There's one thing JP does that's very impactful. And I don't know many men who do this. He spends a week every year at a cabin alone and does an inventory of the previous year. You know, he has a lot of different moving parts in his life, a lot to review. I assume he uses this process to focus his life's energy. When he comes out of that, he tries to make changes for the next year. I think it's an impressive thing about JP. He really takes the time to evaluate.

With all the things JP has going for him, he keeps moving forward. He wants a life that is continually expanding and creating, a life that he loves to engage in, no matter how old he is or where he is. He's not constrained by location or any type of business. He has a kind of all-engulfing, very expansive, very creative kind of charged life. I love that he's a perpetual optimist. He believes in life energy. He's always trying to pick people up and carry them forward. And he loves connecting and communicating. John Paul started out with nothing and he's proof that the American Dream is not dead.

Chapter 24
What's Next?

In my life there's no time for retirement. Let's say you've lived your life as best you can. If you're in your fifties, sixties or seventies and are bored, there's still a lot more you can do. I'm in my eighties; however, I feel like thirty, and I don't plan on ever retiring.

Why do I do it? I think it's fun. Do I need the money? No. But there are lots of things I can do with that money. And I still have plans for the future. Of course, I'll continue to expand on some of what I've already started, whether it's improving John Paul Mitchell Systems or giving people a boost out of poverty, hunger, and homelessness. Number one is my family, of course. I like to know if there's anything my family really needs and deserves that I haven't given them. My friends too.

I'm also planning new things. As I look at my life over the next ten, twenty, thirty or fifty years (some of what I'm working on will improve my health and longevity), I want to continue to help people. I want to change the world by making it a better place to live in, and I want to spread *peace, love and happiness* everywhere.

Hospitality

I'm already in the hospitality business in a big way. I like doing nice luxury developments that make people feel really special as well as my homes for the homeless and for low-income families. Working with Discovery Land Company makes a difference because they share my concern for developments that are ecologically sound. I'm proud of the new communities we're building in Austin, Costa Rica, Barbuda and Montana, as well as the restoration of Taymouth Castle in Scotland.

Of course, my work in Barbuda isn't finished yet. We're planning to build bigger artificial reefs there and we're trying to get that done right on the island instead of importing them from Florida. The amazing community we are building continues to grow and will provide a lot of jobs and economic support to the people of Barbuda.

Who knows where I'll be able to make a difference next?

A Legacy of Peace, Love & Happiness

When I think about my legacy of giving, I think about the seeds that have been planted, literally and metaphorically, in Appalachia through our backyard gardens program at Grow Appalachia. When you help someone grow a garden, whether it's helping them till the dirt or giving them seeds, you are changing the earth. When people are active in growing food for their families, they are out in the sunshine and connected to the land and each other.

I think about the work teams at Chrysalis in LA, the artists at the Entrepreneur Hub at Mobile Loaves & Fishes and the tradespeople at John Paul DeJoria Skills Center at The

Other Ones Foundation in Austin. I have some beautiful art in my home made by artists at the Entrepreneur Hub. People who are homeless have the ability to give to our society. We shouldn't count them out. Giving people a hand up and not a handout makes us all successful.

I think about veterans of all kinds sitting around a fire pit at Patriots' Hall of Dripping Springs, sharing stories and getting resources for their healthcare and for their families.

I think about many children in Mali being able to go to the well outside his or her school to drink and collect water before going to class in the JP's Peace, Love & Happiness School.

I have made a lot of different investments in charities all over the world, but I think what all these organizations and regions that I have chosen to invest in have in common is that they are sometimes in places unseen or written off by our society—Appalachians, Malians, the homeless, veterans. I am a veteran and was twice homeless. I know what that's like. I believe that everyone has something to give. When people have what they need, when people become successful, they share their success too. Giving is something you pass on to others with the hope that they can become givers too. It's contagious. I believe in it so much that I made it the title of this book.

Future Communications

With my pal and partner, the super-scientist, Hal Puthoff, (he helped co-develop remote viewing for the CIA), we're developing technology to deliver sound through walls or mountains.

Future Medicine

I expect to be getting more into the natural and advanced medical businesses in the future. This means perhaps coming up with natural, non-toxic combinations that take the place of chemicals.

One of the companies I'm involved with, together with Dr. Gerard Housey, is working on therapeutic treatments for diabetes (type 1 and 2), cancer, neurodegenerative diseases (dementia, Parkinsons), obesity, and on drug recovery platform technology.

Another company, with Dr. Thom Lobe, is working on a combination therapy for increasing NAD levels and migrating CD38 inhibitors. They potentially enhance mitochondrial function.

And yet another company is working on human longevity. My friend and super-cool business associate, Kim Shafer, is doing ground-breaking work with super probiotics . . . Daily Body Restore . . . a leader in the industry.

Clean Water

I am now partnered with two companies that have found the answer to clean water, including inexpensively removing salt from sea water.

ROKiT

In 2018, my family trust through investment, co-founded the ROKiT Group of companies with business partner, JK Since then, we have created brands such as ROKiT Phones,

ROKiT Telemedicine, ROKiT Drinks, ROKiT Homes, and more. If you check our website, here's what you'll see: *We like to do things differently. Through compassionate capitalism, we strive to deliver affordable, world leading premium products and pioneering services for all. We take our products, partnerships and responsibilities very seriously but never ourselves. We are innovative, rebellious and proud.* We are kind, fair, rebellious and we look into something to be proud of. That kind of sums up my philosophy about life and business.

ROKiT is expanding to transportation, energy opportunities and fashion. With our new partnership with BMW, we are also expanding into motorcycles, tires, and specialty products. We have partnerships with major manufacturers.

Renew Logic and Vendidit

This is my biggest project right now and I'm so excited about it. I met Gary Stephens with Justin in 2015 and he told me about his reverse logistics company. What's reverse logistics? It's the supply chain process in which products are returned from the point of sale to the manufacturer or distributor for recovery, repair, recycling, or disposal. You may not know this, but when you return most products to a store, whether it's an iPhone or a pair of shoes, the store can't put it back on the shelf. They have to write off the cost and then find a way to dispose of it. Traditionally, products go into a warehouse where they can sit for up to two years before a solution is found. Eventually, they are redistributed through a reverse logistics company for use elsewhere. The challenge is to avoid putting the products in landfills. There are so many big companies with this problem that some of them send their returned products to China and elsewhere where they are put in landfills anyway.

Gary knew I was into renewing or reusing products to prevent damage to the environment. He had the technology to buy the returned merchandise (they handle everything but food), disassemble (if necessary), keep the parts that are valuable, re-market those products, and recycle the rest with ecology in mind. I thought it was a brilliant idea so I decided to partner with him and Justin and we decided to call it Renew Logic. Best decision I could have made. Gary is a go-getter and a very caring human being.

From Gary Stephens

My story is similar to John Paul's in a way. I was living out of my car and on people's couches. Before that, I had a fantastic professional career, made a lot of money, but I lost it all through a divorce and a series of bad decisions and got myself into an almost hopeless position. I had to decide if I was going to be a victim of my own circumstances or some sort of phoenix rising from the ashes. I chose the phoenix. So, I grabbed myself by the bootstraps and rebuilt my life.

When I met JP, our energies aligned perfectly. Every time I was around him was like getting a B-12 shot. Turns out we had that effect on each other. John Paul DeJoria is the light of positivity in my life. He lit my torch and made me feel like life is worth living. Now I can give it back to him so he can help others too.

I knew my reverse logistics business was already having a positive impact on the environment when we got into electronics.

After a while, we started refurbishing and recycling computers for the big companies like Dell, Lenovo and HP. That's when JP came on board as a partner, and we launched Renew Logic.

After a few years of partnering with Renew Logic, Gary came up with a new idea. He explained that we had some big accounts but by the time we got the merchandise it had passed through many other people and that cost a lot of money. Let's say a big retailer gets a whole bunch of stuff returned. They write it off as a loss and send it to a giant warehouse which also costs money. Every time a product gets touched or moved; it's costing that company more. After a while—sometimes it's a year or two—the products are finally examined or tested and then some are sold to a reverse logistics company at a much lower cost. The reverse logistics company then finds other places where the products or parts can be sold—again, for an even lower price.

The original retailer loses a lot of money in unusable returned merchandise, not to mention the cost of shipping and warehousing. I know one good-sized company that loses two hundred million dollars a year in returned products. Gary told me he believed that no company in our space had a platform that could help either a manufacturer with overruns or a retailer with returns make any of that money back. Then he told me something amazing. He'd discovered a way for companies to make a profit and sell their product directly from business to business. I thought his idea was brilliant.

We called it Vendidit (from the Latin word to sell) and it's growing quickly.

From Gary Stephens

With Renew Logic, we'd started to develop some smart technology and smart processes and procedures for dealing with the material we were getting. That brings us to our new company. We developed a software platform we called Apex. It was so good at processing information that we knew how we were going to route material before it even hit our facility. We were able to determine the value and the ability to predict the best use and redistribution channels for returned merchandise.

Ten months later, we had something that was both functioning and functional.

Changing Life in the City

With my partners, Mike Lance and Matt Samwick, we have a development in Washington State where we are moving the entire town center to a new location. It will be a multi-purpose town center within walking distance of new homes, businesses, stores, markets, and transportation . . . with ecology in mind. Over the years, Eloise, John Anthony and I have traveled to many parts of the planet on adventures with Mike, his wonderful wife Deborah, and their family. We've been to Machu Picchu, the deep parts of the Amazon, New Zealand, the Galápagos Islands, and more. It's been so much fun doing business with friends.

Sharing My Voice

My voice makes a difference these days. That's why I try to accept a few invitations to speak to groups. If I can get my message out to thousands or even millions of people, I'll do it. Telling people how to succeed by being positive, serving as an example, and investing money to good causes is all part of my "Success Unshared is Failure" philosophy. I want to expand good fortune for others. And now, I can change the world with what I've accomplished. There's no better feeling!

My Rituals

When I go to bed at night, I always give gratitude. I say, "Creator of Souls, thank you for this incredible, happy life you've given me. I really appreciate it and hope I do really good, because I am the presence of your action in me."

When I wake up in the morning . . . before I jump into my day . . . I try, for about five minutes, just to *be.* I think about how I want the day to be positive, I want to help others, and I want to be the observer without judgment. Thank you, universe, for this beautiful day you're giving me.

Then I look at my life, I look at my schedule (which I've done the night before), and see when I'm going to have a little bit of time for myself. And then, I immediately get up, go to the window, and look outside. I look around and it makes me feel good. Other than that, I just go about my day. I have so many things going for me at the same time and I'm really happy about it.

I try twice a year to have a few days all by myself, go to the mountains, look at what's happening in my life now that

I like. I look at where I don't want to be or who I want to be around. I look forward to starting a new year getting more negativity off the table and how I can make the new year even better than the last.

I go to the mountains for three days and two nights to reflect and clear my head. It gives me focus.

Chapter 25

My Legacy

I'd like to thank you for reading my story, and I'd like to thank my friends and family for adding their thoughts. I hope you've enjoyed it all. It's brought back a lot of memories. In spite of the ups and downs in my life, I've always tried to stay positive.

When someone is talking about me in the future, I hope they'll say something like this:

He was a kind man who paid his rent for being here in many ways on our beautiful earth. He built businesses which were good for the planet, hired a whole lot of people, taught kindness in management, and tried to be over-the-top fair with everyone. He helped people who didn't have work to get back to the workplace by caring about them personally, and he built homes for those who needed them. He gave money to charities, but he also showed up and encouraged those in need, helped the planet, and a lot of people had better lives because he was here.

John Paul DeJoria loved his life and friends. He got his high from doing nice things for other people. He showed us that "Success Unshared is Failure" is a lesson for every human being and that nothing will get you higher than when you do something for somebody else and ask for nothing in return—not even a thank you.

And above all, JP lived a life of JOY—always finding the positive in anything and everyone he touched!

So be kind, unite with others worldwide to fight hunger and poverty, safeguard our planet, and give hope to children in need. And remember: Nothing in life is worth doing unless you're having fun doing it.

Peace, Love, Happiness, and Kindness to all of you.

My Favorite Quotes

These are some of my favorite *Words To Live By* (some are mine; some are inspiration from others).

"Success Unshared is Failure."

"Successful people do all the things unsuccessful people do not want to do."

"Pay attention to the vital few, and ignore the trivial many."

"The two most important things in your life are your health and your happiness: if you have those, everything else can fall into place."

"Pay kindness forward. A kind gesture can change someone's day . . . or their world."

"Don't be in the selling business, be in the reorder business (a service or product they want to keep using)."

"Be prepared for rejection . . . be as enthusiastic on Door #101 as you were on Door #1."

"When you lose, don't lose the lesson, too."

"Giving but expecting nothing in return is the greatest high you'll ever experience."

"Most people tiptoe through life to make it safely to death."

"When the going gets tough, the tough get going."

"Be the observer . . . without judgement . . . or you pull it
into your universe."

"Remember the customer is always right, even if they're
wrong, to them they are right."

"In the end everything will be ok . . . and if it's not ok
. . . it's not the end."

"Smile as much as possible, you can help
change the world!"

"When you do what you love, it's not work."

"Part of what you earn is yours to keep:
every time you get paid, take five-ten percent before you
pay any bills and put that away in savings."

"Reprimand in private, praise in public."

"Kindness is one of the free secrets of a
successful and happy life."

"Worrying is like praying for something
you don't want."

"Which is more important,
the journey or the destination?"

"It's the company along the way . . .
and when you arrive."

"The secret to love . . . is . . . to love thyself . . .
otherwise love does not exist."

My Notes

I could not have written this book alone, and I'm grateful to everyone who has been involved. First, thank you to Gail Fink who was the one who started me on the journey to writing my story. Thank you to Mark, Crystal, Carol, and the amazing team at MVHL who guided and advised me so incredibly and brought this book to life.

Thank you to everyone who added to my story with their own words and insights. And a big thank you to Anne and my inside team (you know who you are!) who thoughtfully read and offered input as this book developed. I truly value your insights and suggestions!

This book is built on my recollections and interpretations of my life and events in it. I have attempted to be as factually accurate as possible, but any errors or discrepancies are my own. I know I've been blessed to have had such a full and bountiful life. There are many other amazing people, notable moments, and wonderful memories from my life that are not in this book but still hold special places in my heart.

Some of the Special People Who Have Done Special Things

A special thank you to Eloise, my yellow rose of Texas, who is as beautiful inside as she is on the outside . . . and our entire family. I am so blessed to have the family I do . . . you have supported me and stood by me over so many years . . . I love you all so much!

Roger Daltry—my friend of many decades who brought the band with him to entertain at my wedding as a gift to Eloise and me. During the event, Cher jumped on the stage and sang a few songs with them . . . It was magic! Roger also gave me the key to his castle in Sussex, England.

Dan Aykroyd—my friend who narrated my documentary movie *Good Fortune* as a gift and who was also my Patrón distributor in Canada. While we were opening up the House of Blues, we had many great motorcycle rides together. A dear friend and business associate.

John and Doris Capra—John has been one of my first best friends for over 50 years . . . he's seen me through thick and thin and has always been there to lend a hand. The two of them have some of the biggest hearts in the world and I love them dearly.

Pierce and Keely Brosnan—great friends who are always there to better the planet and the lives of all the people on it.

Walter and Diana Staudinger—two of my best buddies.

Always positive and full of exciting stories . . . great fun in both our personal lives and business ventures.

Bill Shaffer—my biker and car pal who has helped me in so many ways over so many years, never asking anything in return.

Willie Nelson—never ever too big for his britches despite being one of the iconic voices of our time. One year, for my birthday, he sent a short video of a song he wrote about me. Eloise and I have also had the privilege of dining with Willie and his beautiful wife, Annie. Thank you, Willie and Annie.

Tony Robbins—who brought me on as guest speaker in two of his master seminars. He also so graciously was my guest speaker for one of my big Paul Mitchell seminars. Neither of us would accept a speaking fee, we were just good pals helping each other out. We also had a great time spending a week with him on his island in Fiji. A super-good man who cares about the world, and his seminars have helped so many people.

Rick Perry—a great guy and former governor of Texas and Secretary of Energy of the United States. Rick rode on his motorcycle with us in our PLH Charity ride while he was still governor. He brought us to France to have a small, private dinner with the Aga Khan. Today he dedicates most of his time to helping U.S. Veterans with trauma. What a giving human.

Captain Paul Watson—We traveled as shipmates with Alexis to save baby Harp Seals and joined together to save whales, dolphins, and many other marine lives . . . making a difference to life on Planet Earth.

My entire Home Office team—who make my life, and my family's life, so much easier: **Kevin, Paul, Nancy, Tom, Kristen, Jason, Wes, David W, Vicente, Jonathan, David K,**

David R, Justin, Lauren, Gina, Abby, Ashley, Chris, George, Vin, and Gary.

My global super Paul Mitchell family—both present and past . . . I continue to be so proud of what we do, and who we do it for . . . and this company couldn't exist without all of you. We ALL made it happen!

All my friends who come ride motorcycles with us at the PLH Charity ride each April in Austin . . . a super-cool group of humans!

Six hundred of my Ranchero Vistador Brothers, Henry Anderson, Dr. Deborah Brosnan, my ecology partner, Ed and Ashley Brown, Tom Collopy, Ilana Edelstein (author of *The Patrón Way*), **Meena Flynn and her colleagues who helped at Goldman-Sachs, Jimmy Fortescue, Sammy and Kari Hager, Luke and Britta Jacobellis, Michael and Marla Kantor, Jonathan Kendrick, Bobby and Cheryl Kennedy Jr, Rich Kirch, Dennis Marini, Harry and Sandy McDonald, Connelly McGreevy and his team, Mike Meldman, Steven Paul, Johnny Rivers, Rebecca Rothstein, Jennifer Van Kleeck and their team, Larry and Camille Ruvo, Bob Shapiro, Gary and Laurie Spellman, Hadi and Dennis Stein, Josh and Rebecca Tickell, Danny Trejo, Elizabeth Vargas (my pal, co-host, and business partner), and Dolly Parton** . . . with whom I provide books for young children who don't have any.

All my extended family in Zapotal, Barbuda, Taymouth Castle, Driftwood and Territory 1889.

Bob O.—who has kept me accountable for longer than I can remember, and has a heart of gold.

Constance Dykhuizen, who expertly runs JP's Peace, Love & Happiness Family Foundation, making it possible for so many to benefit. **Kelly Sellers**, our longtime personal assistant who is in charge of Getting Things Done. **Brian Kearley**, our assistant of decades. **Anne Germaine**, who is not just my executive assistant but my Chief of Staff. And **Marilyn, Oswaldo, Betty, Dini, and Raudel** . . . who make our home life perfect!

Real pals while they were still in their human bodies—**James Colburn, Paul and Angus Mitchell, Lee Meyer, CB Sullivan, Sir Robert Clegg, John Lee Hooker, BB King, Alan Thicke, Joan Rivers, Dennis Hopper, Peter Fonda, Martin Crowley, and Leslie Spears.**

To our two Ranchero brothers who in the final twilight of their lives . . . with doctors in tow . . . decided to leave their earthly bodies not in a hospital bed, but rather with riding their horses with us . . . their wishes came true . . . RIDE COWBOYS RIDE!!!

John Paul DeJoria

Photo by Estelle Bohl.

John Paul DeJoria epitomizes the American dream, rising from adversity to become a renowned entrepreneur and philanthropist. He is best known for co-founding iconic brands John Paul Mitchell Systems and The Patrón Spirits Company. John Paul has made philanthropy his core mission, establishing JP's Peace, Love & Happiness Family Foundation in 2011 to contribute to a sustainable planet by investing in people, animals, and the environment. His motto, "Success Unshared is Failure," reflects a lifelong commitment to purpose-driven success.